Animal Jungle

ILLUSTRATED: By Lin Watchorn

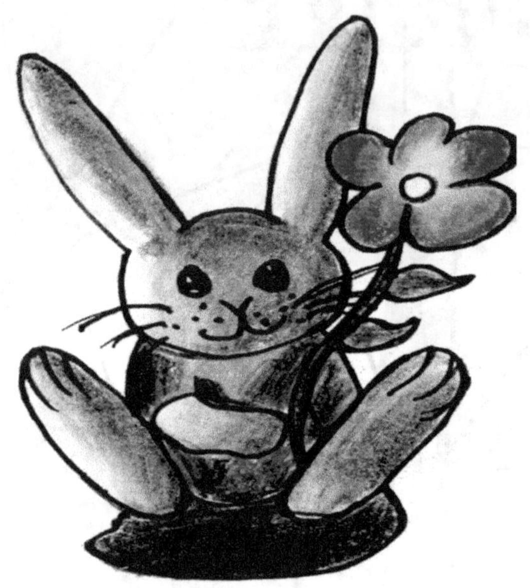

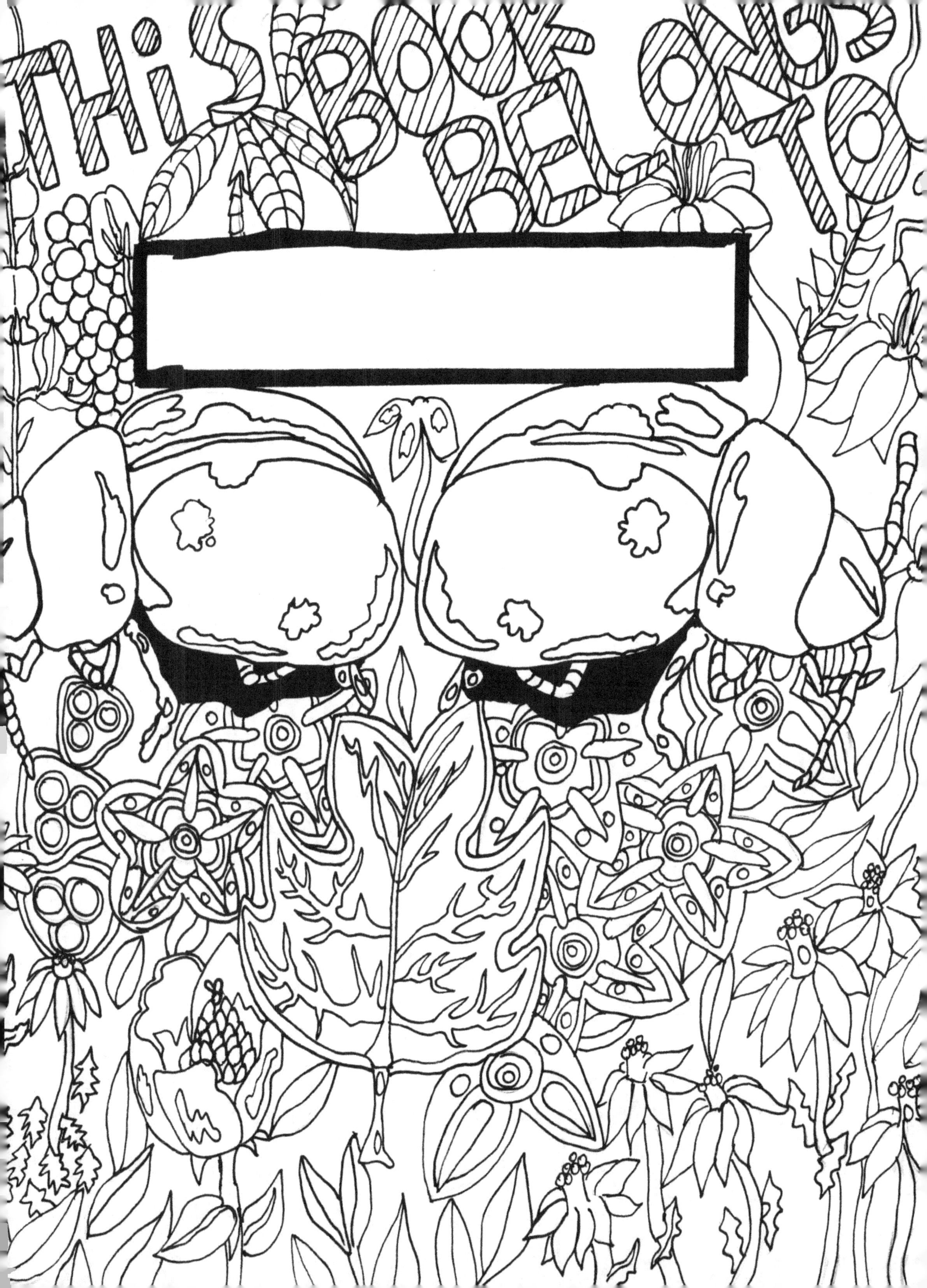

THIS BOOK BELONGS TO

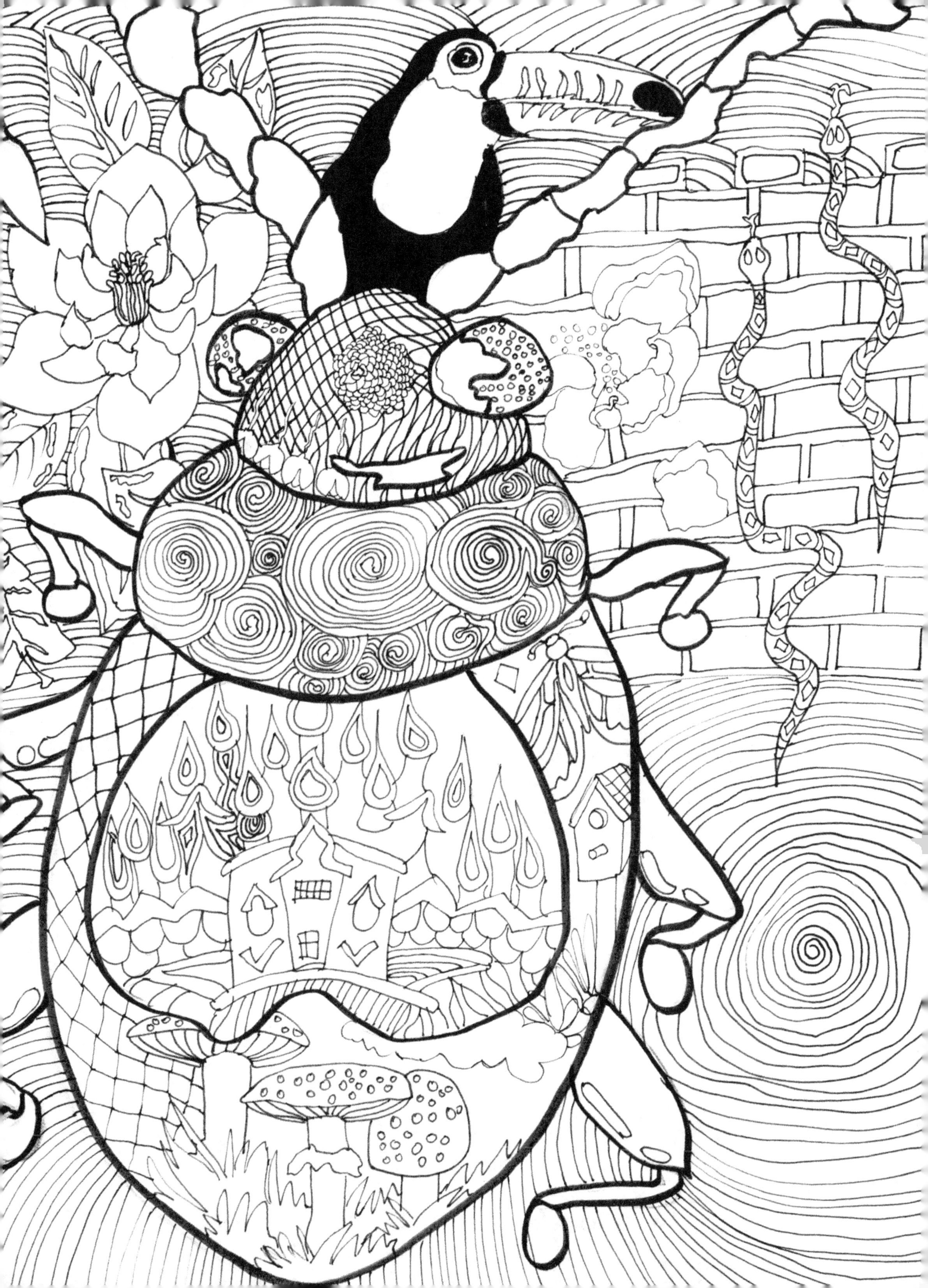

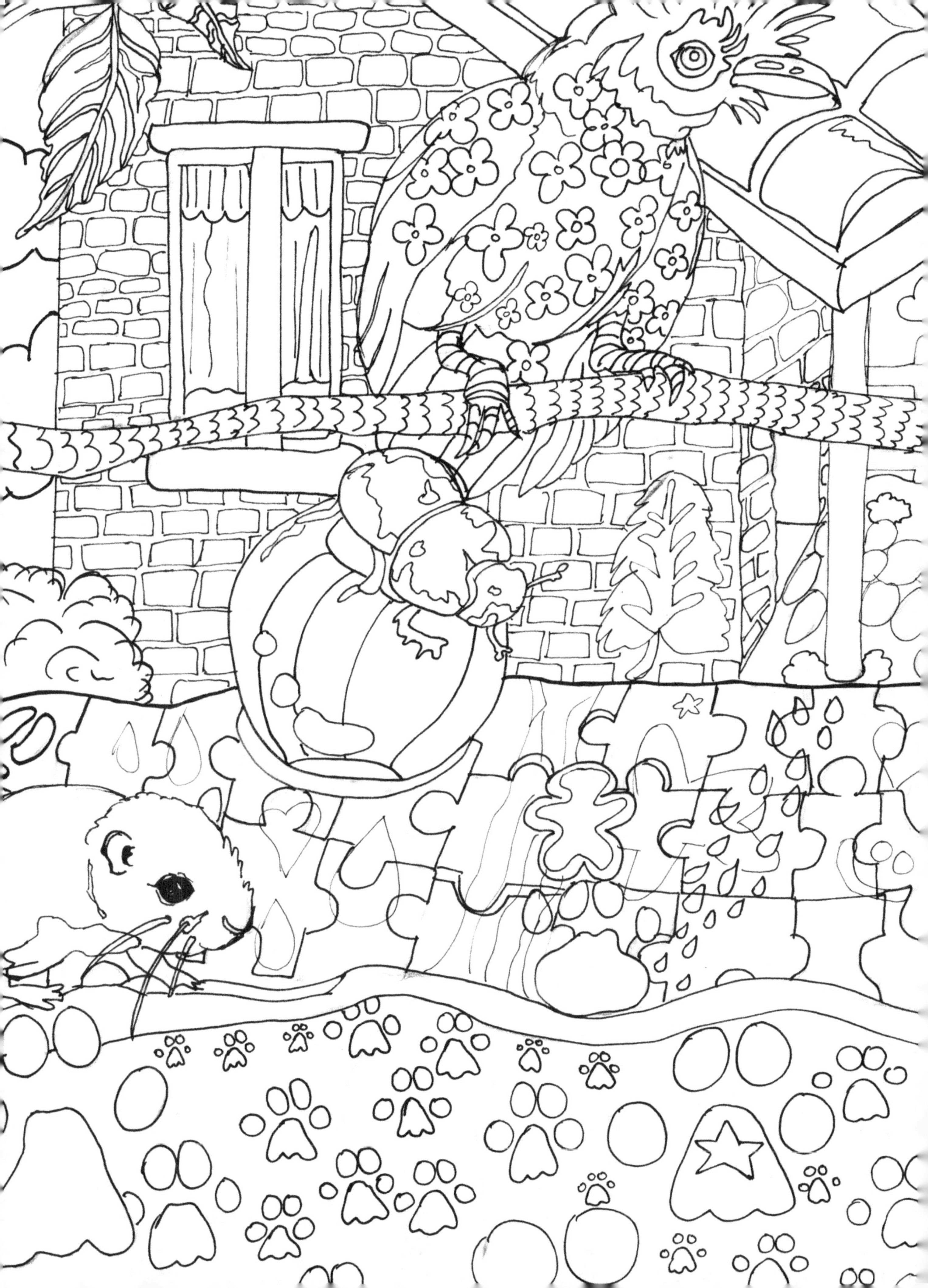

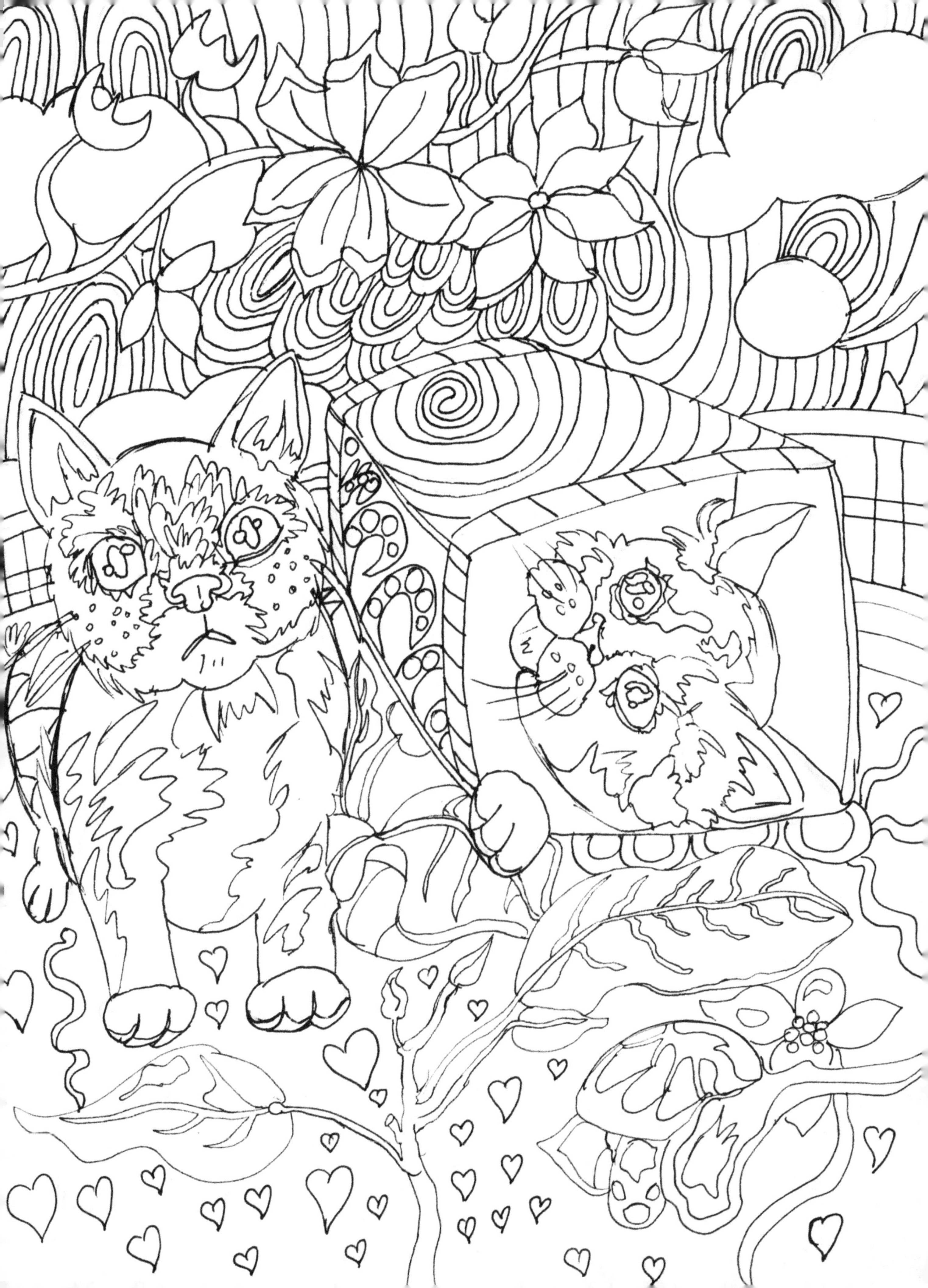

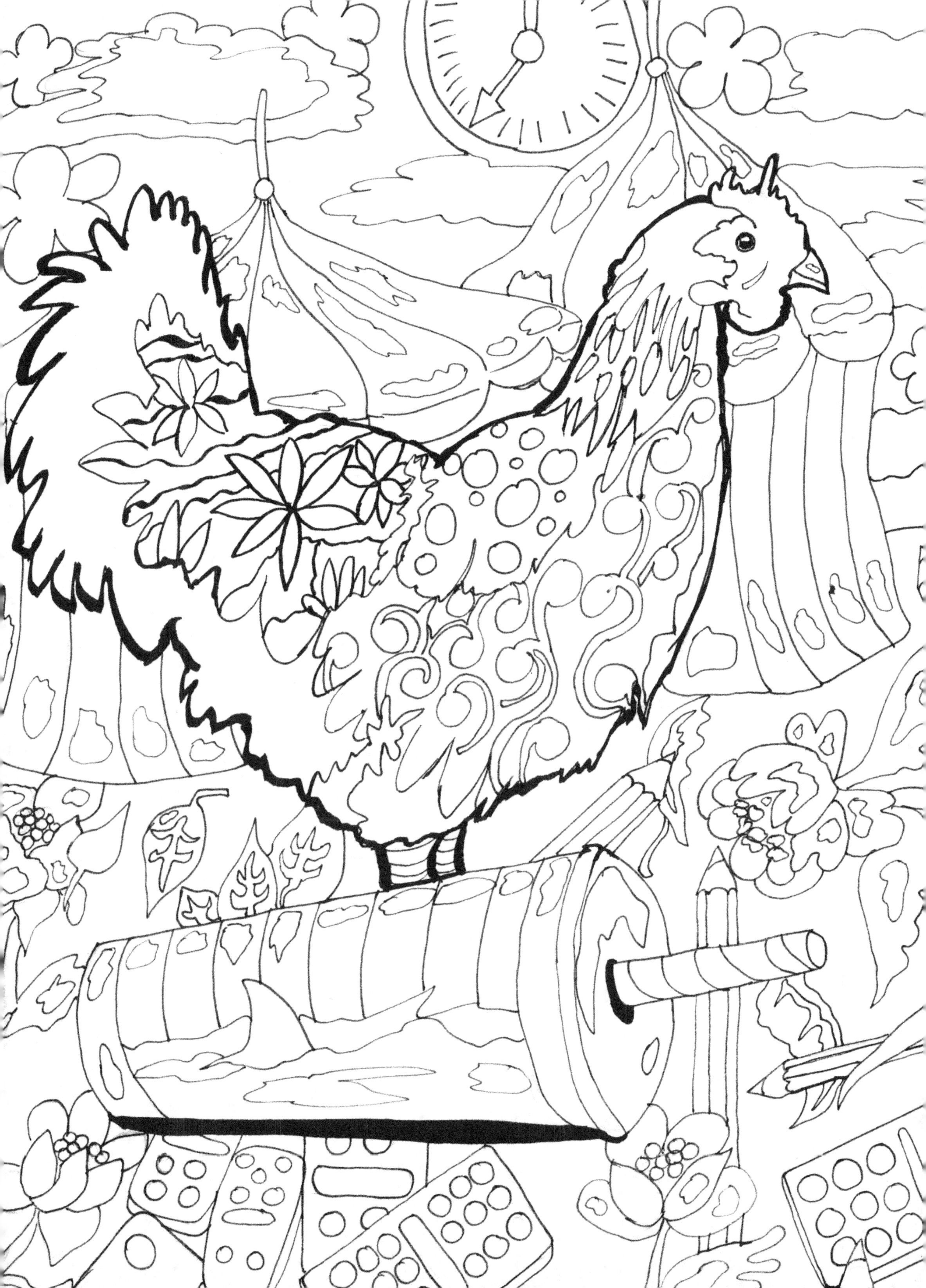

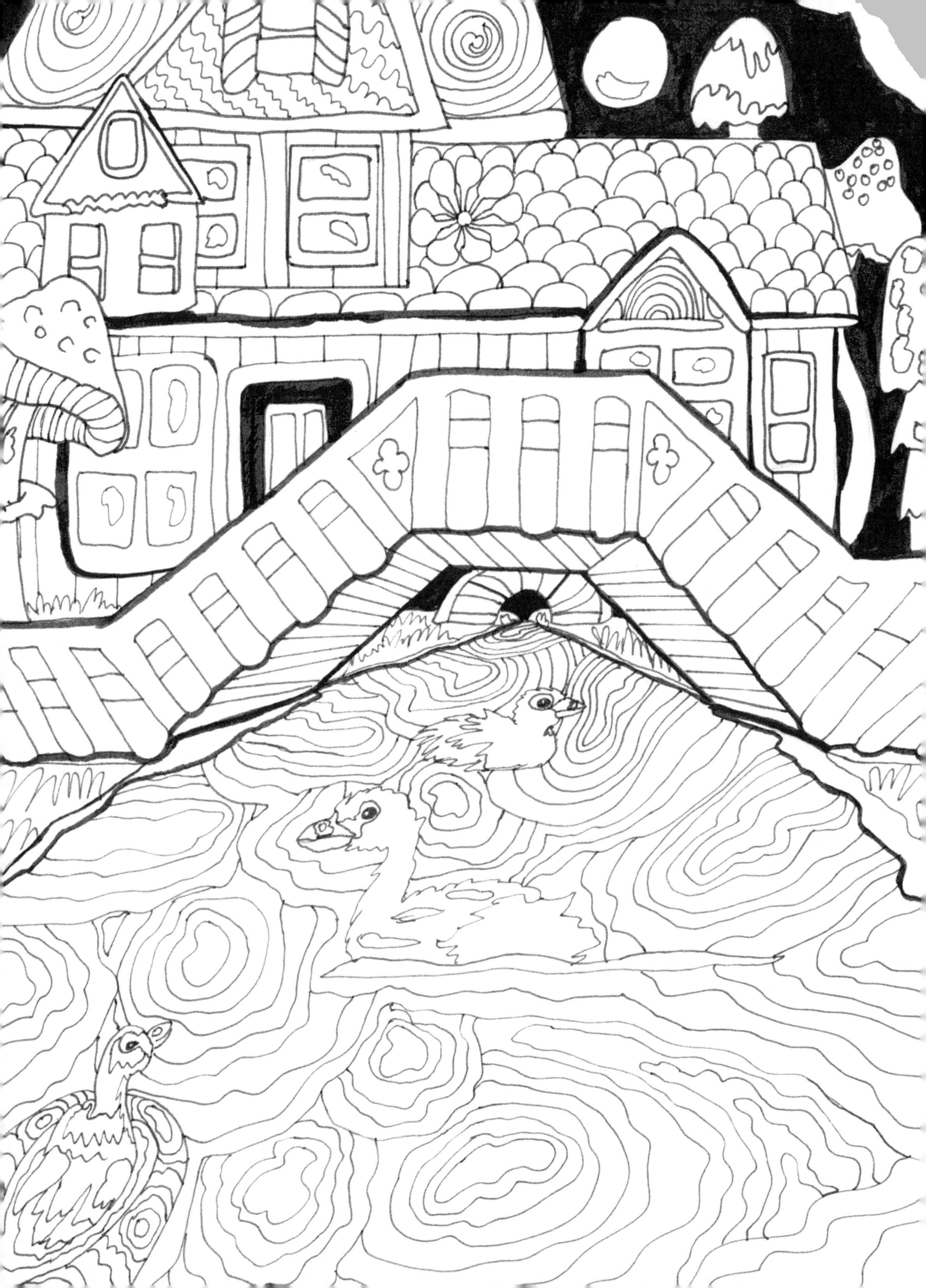

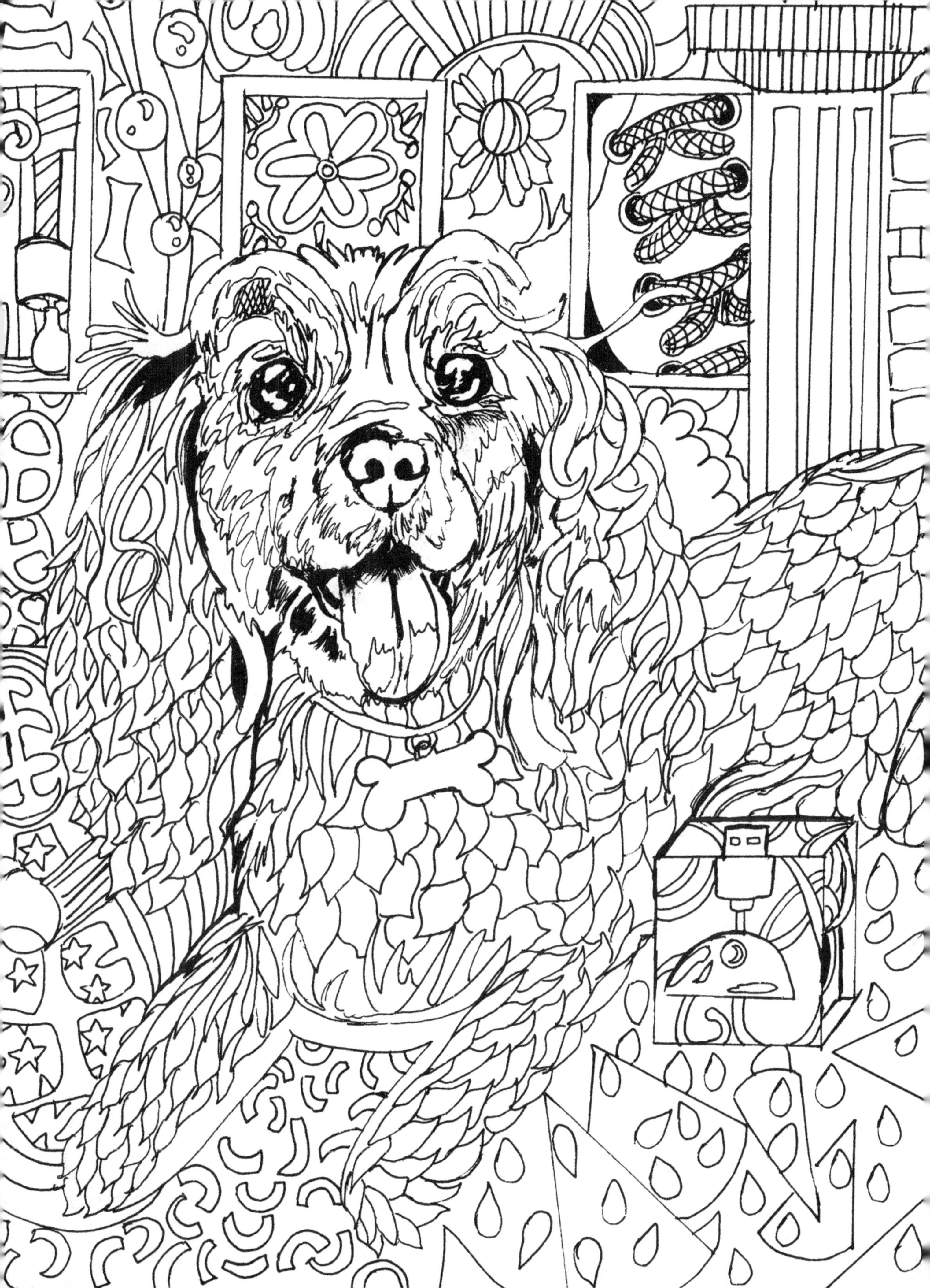

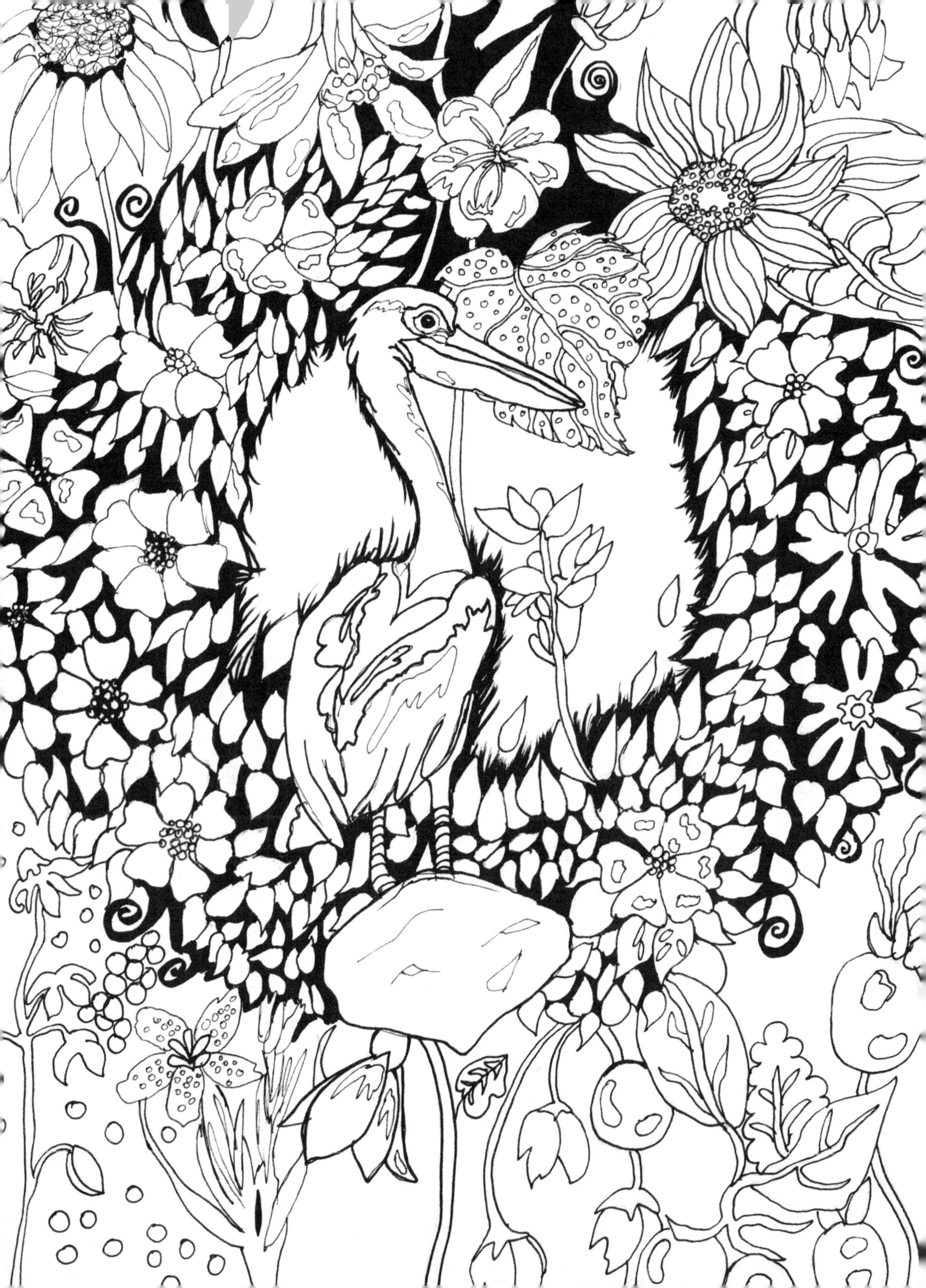

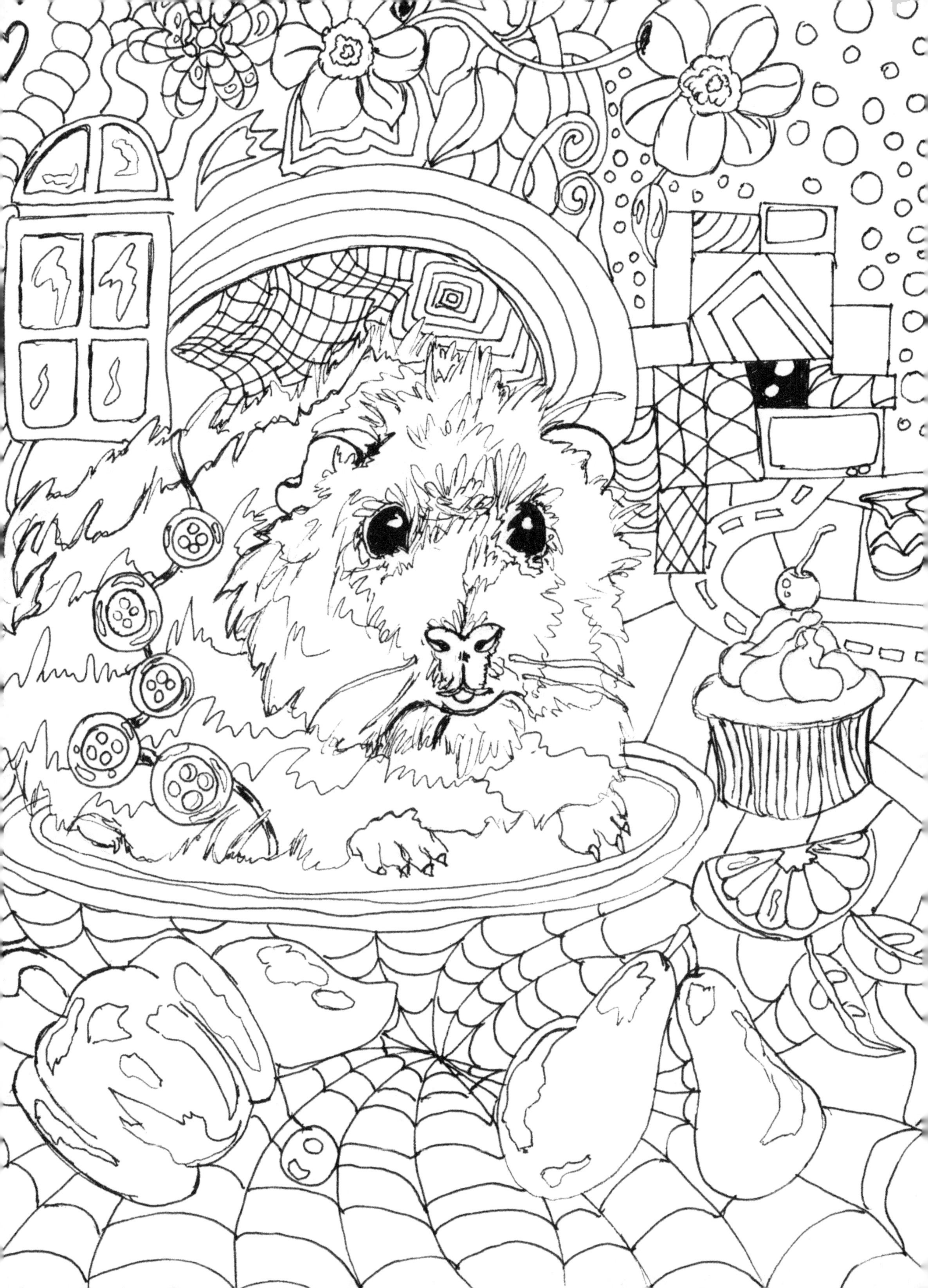

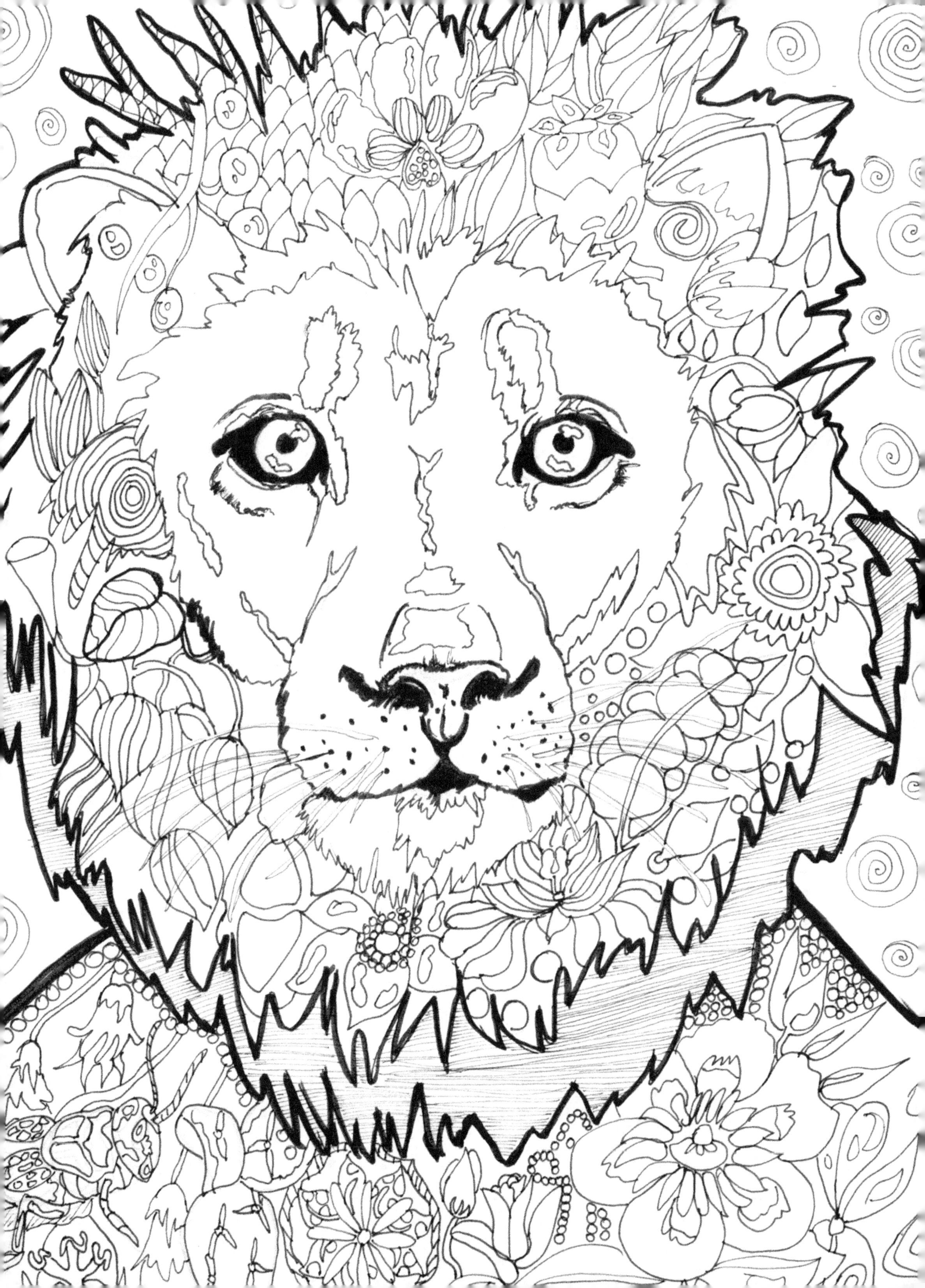

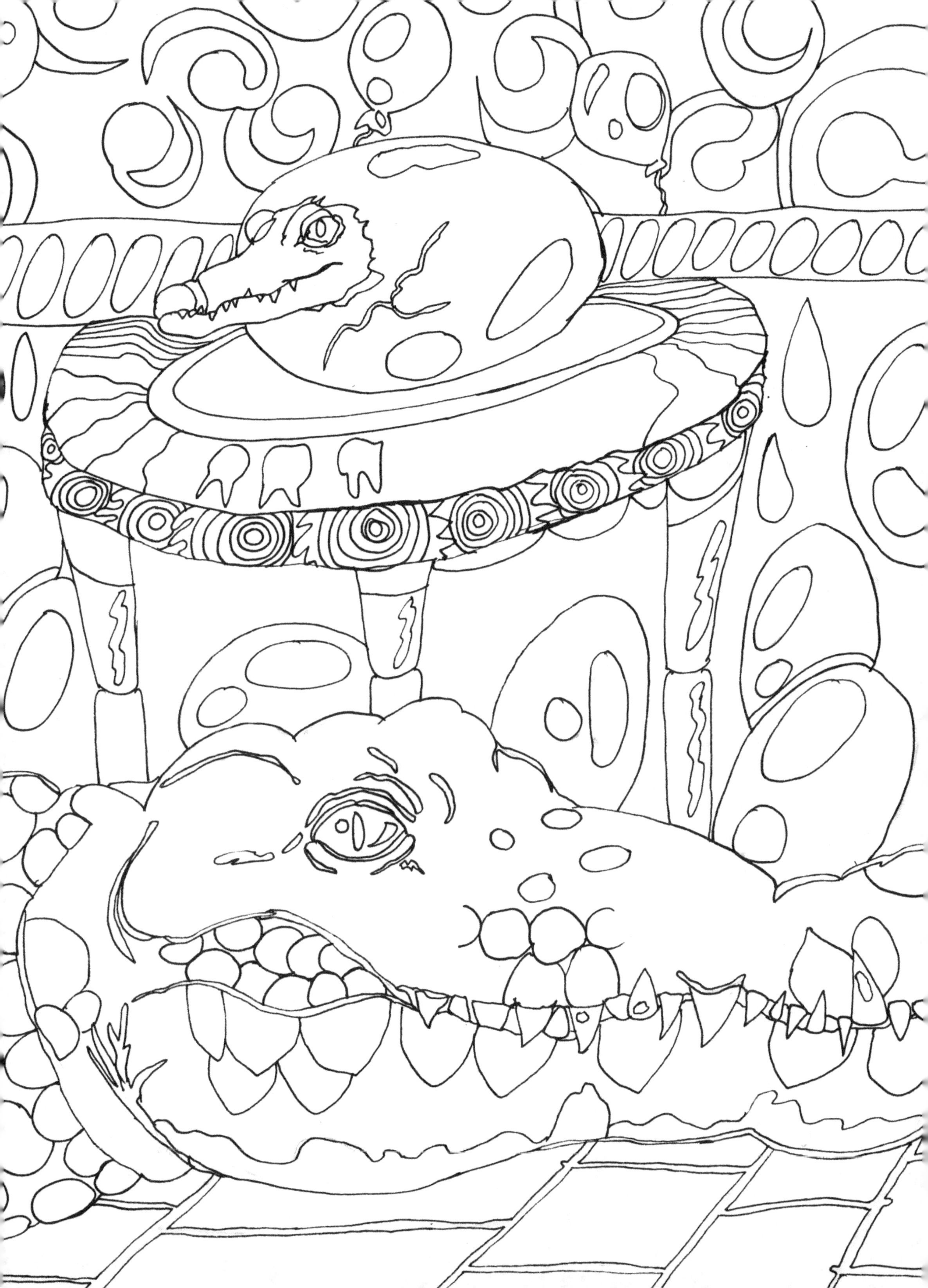

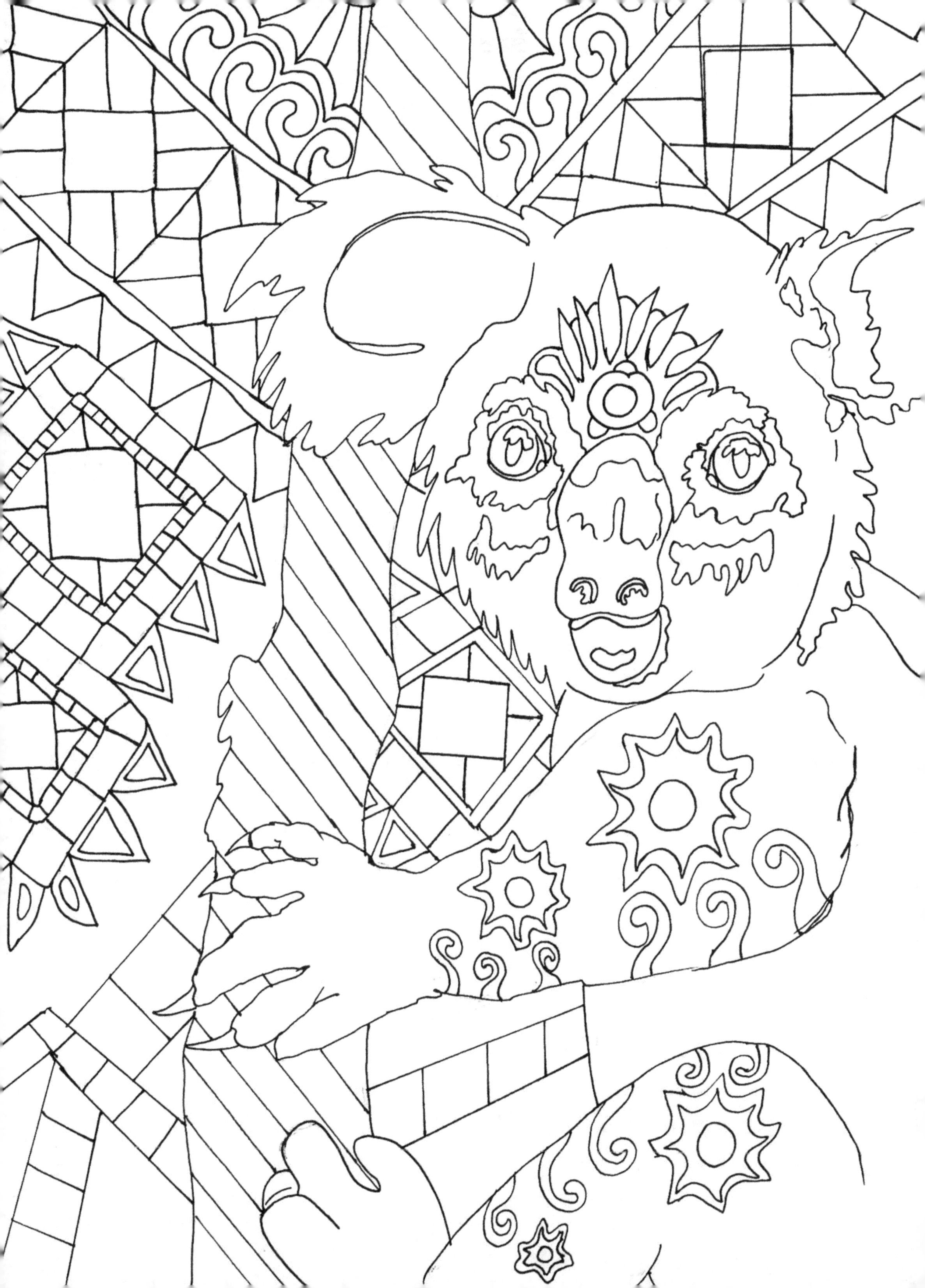

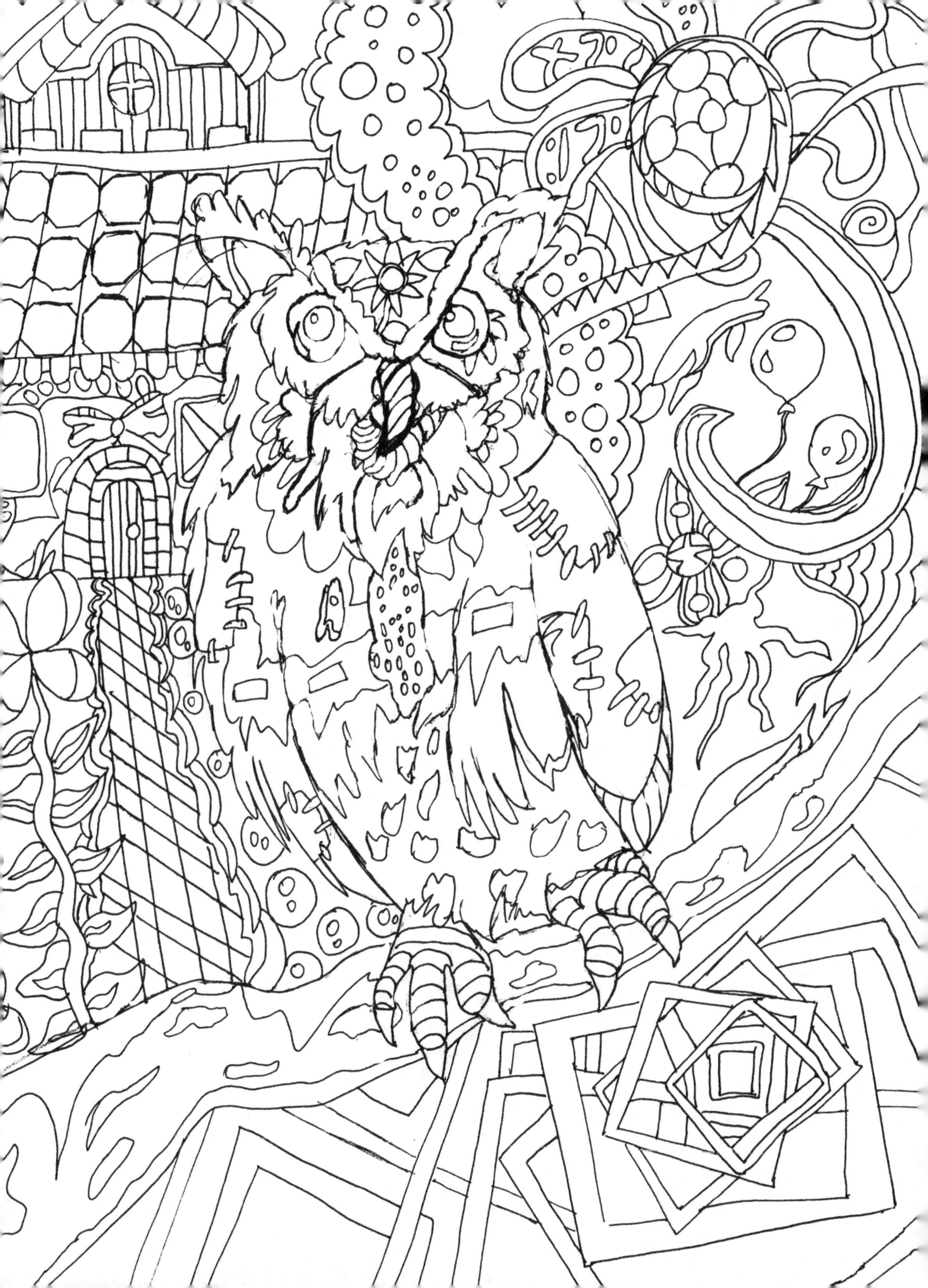

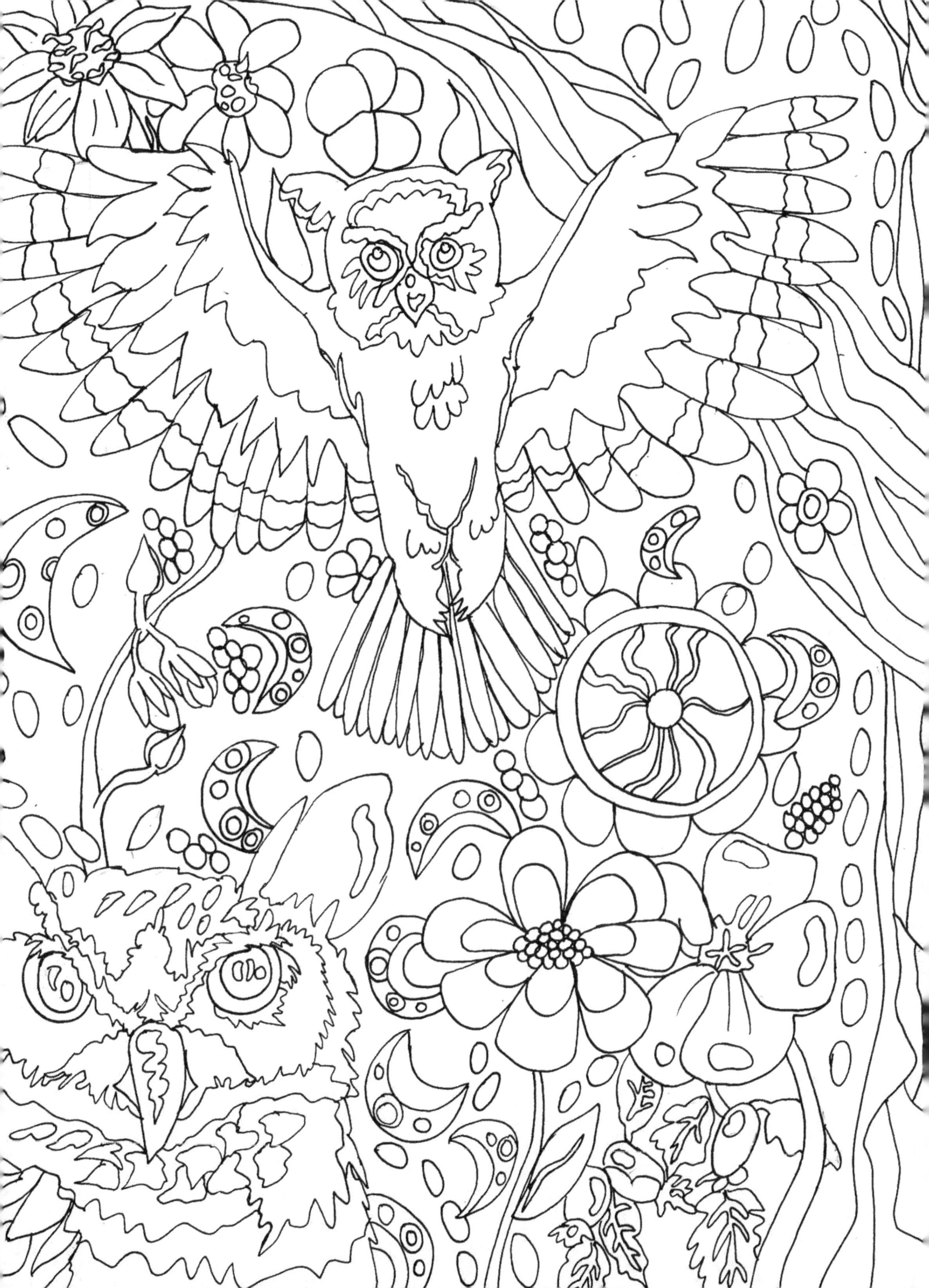

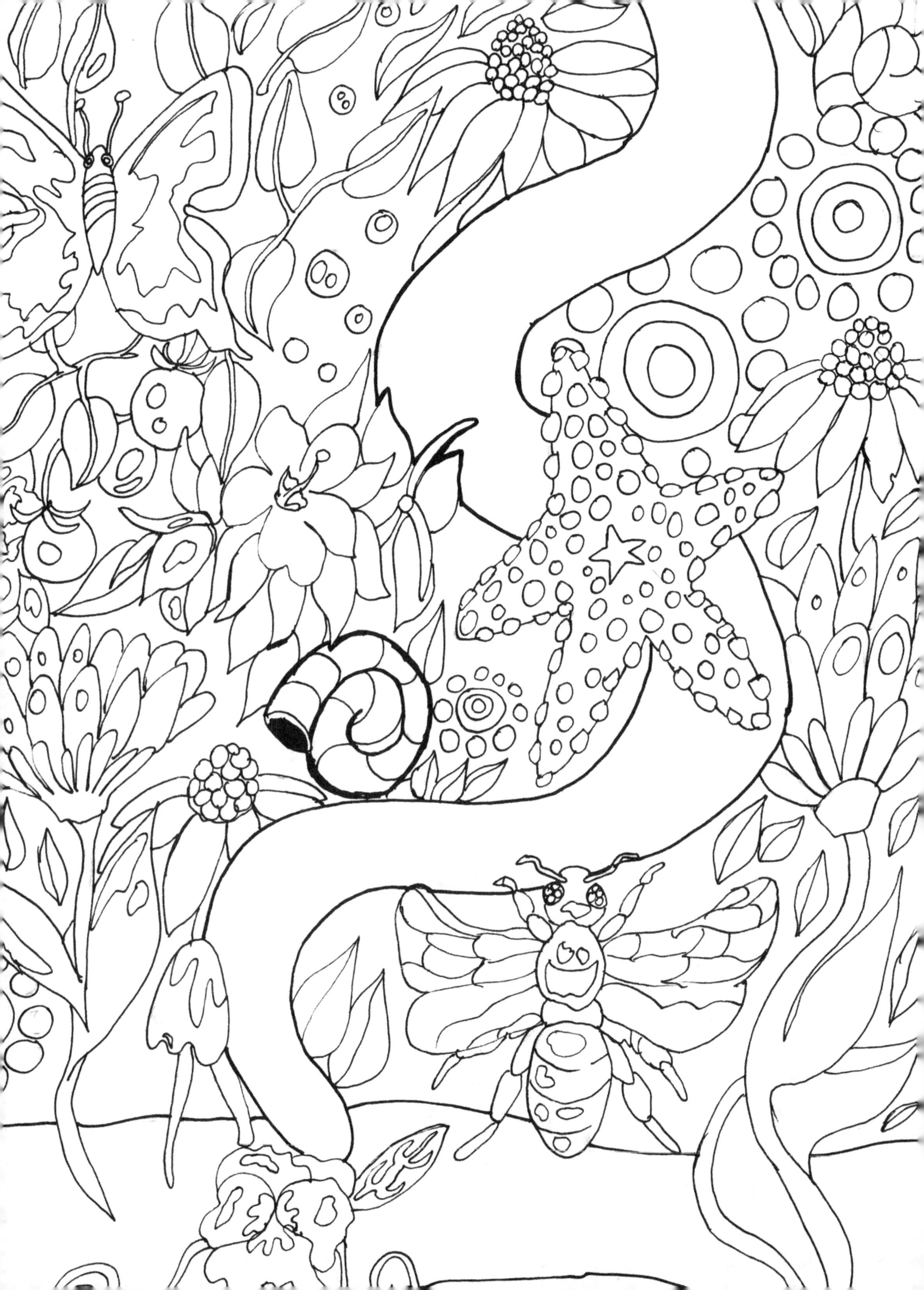

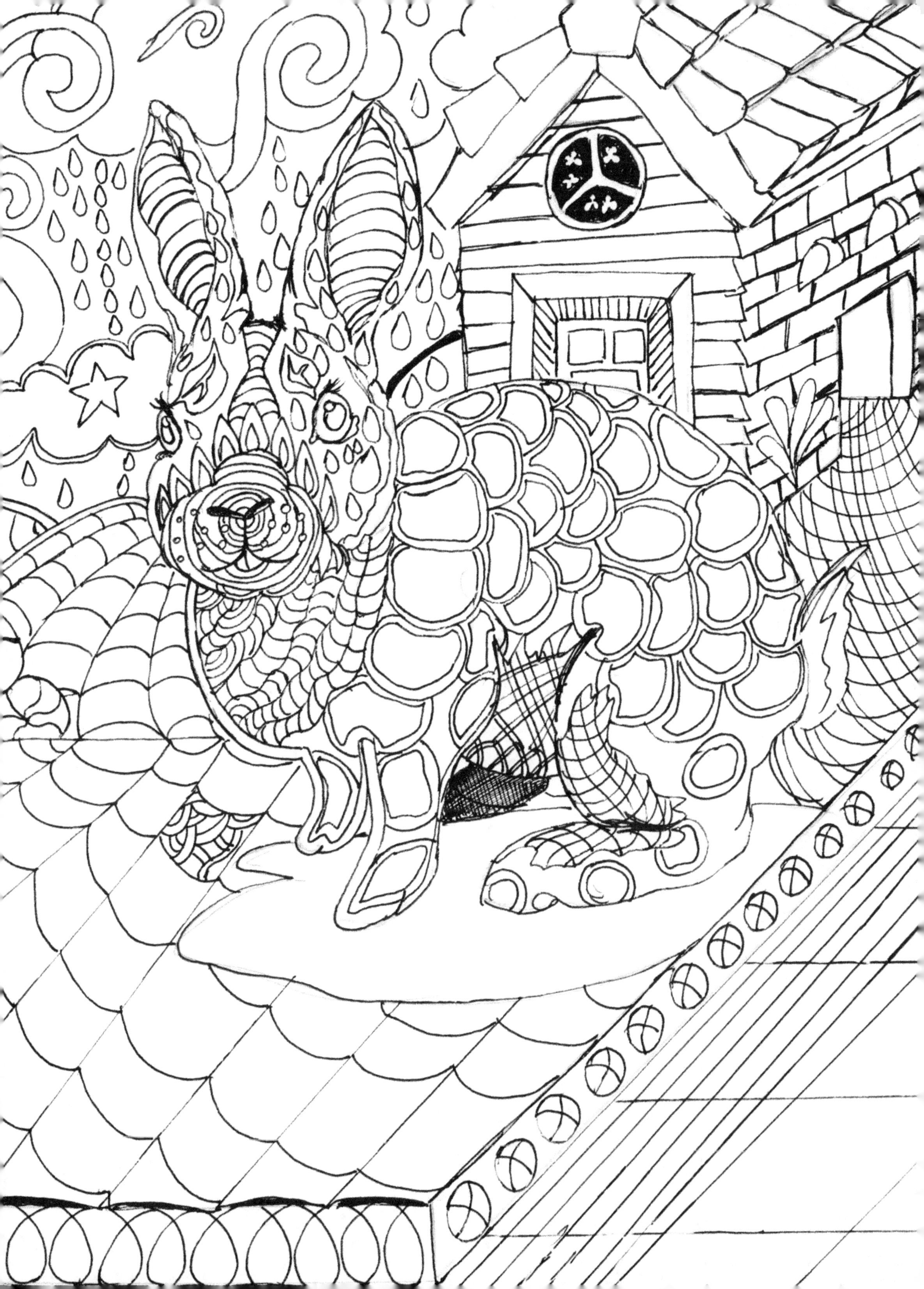

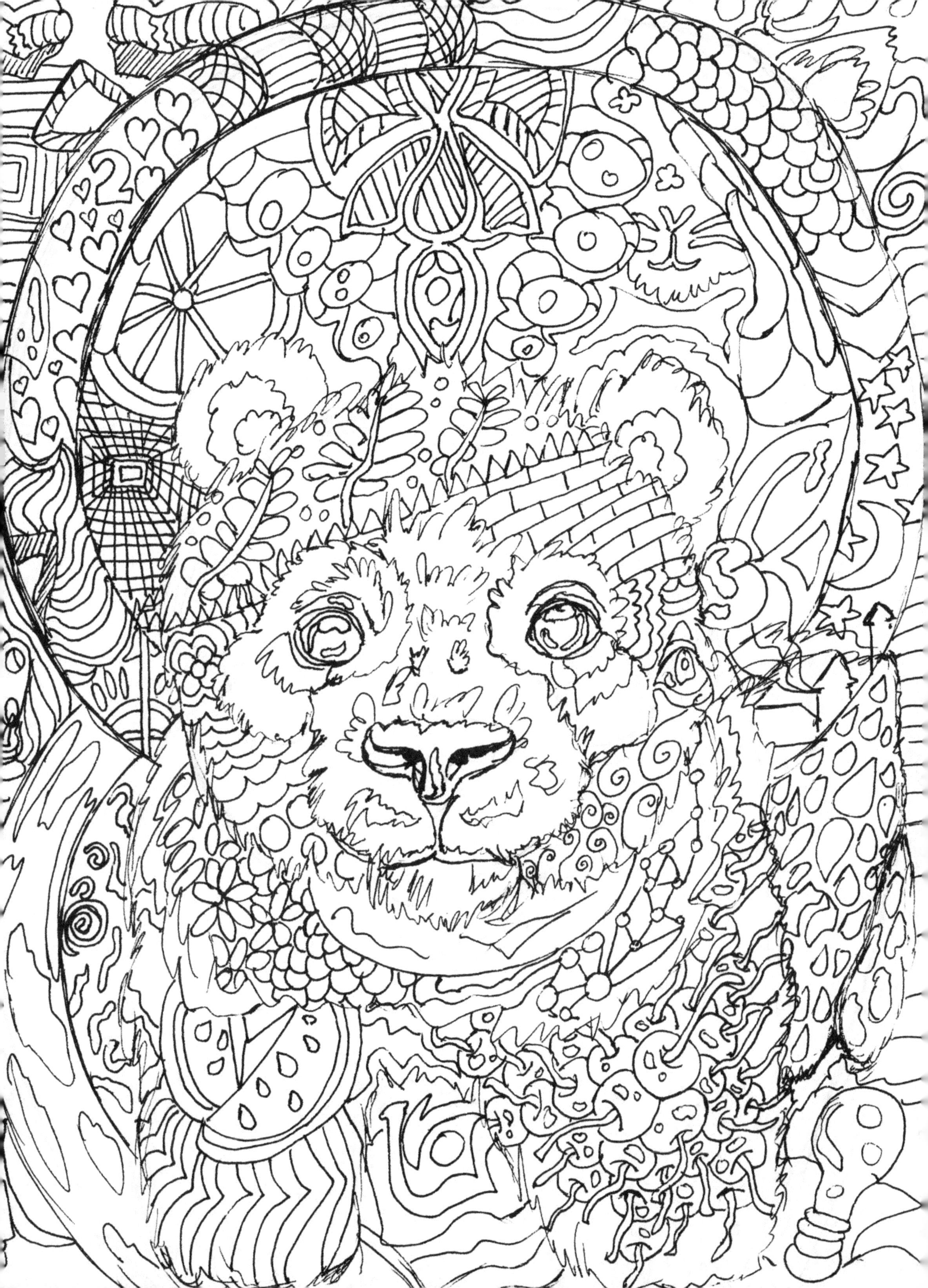

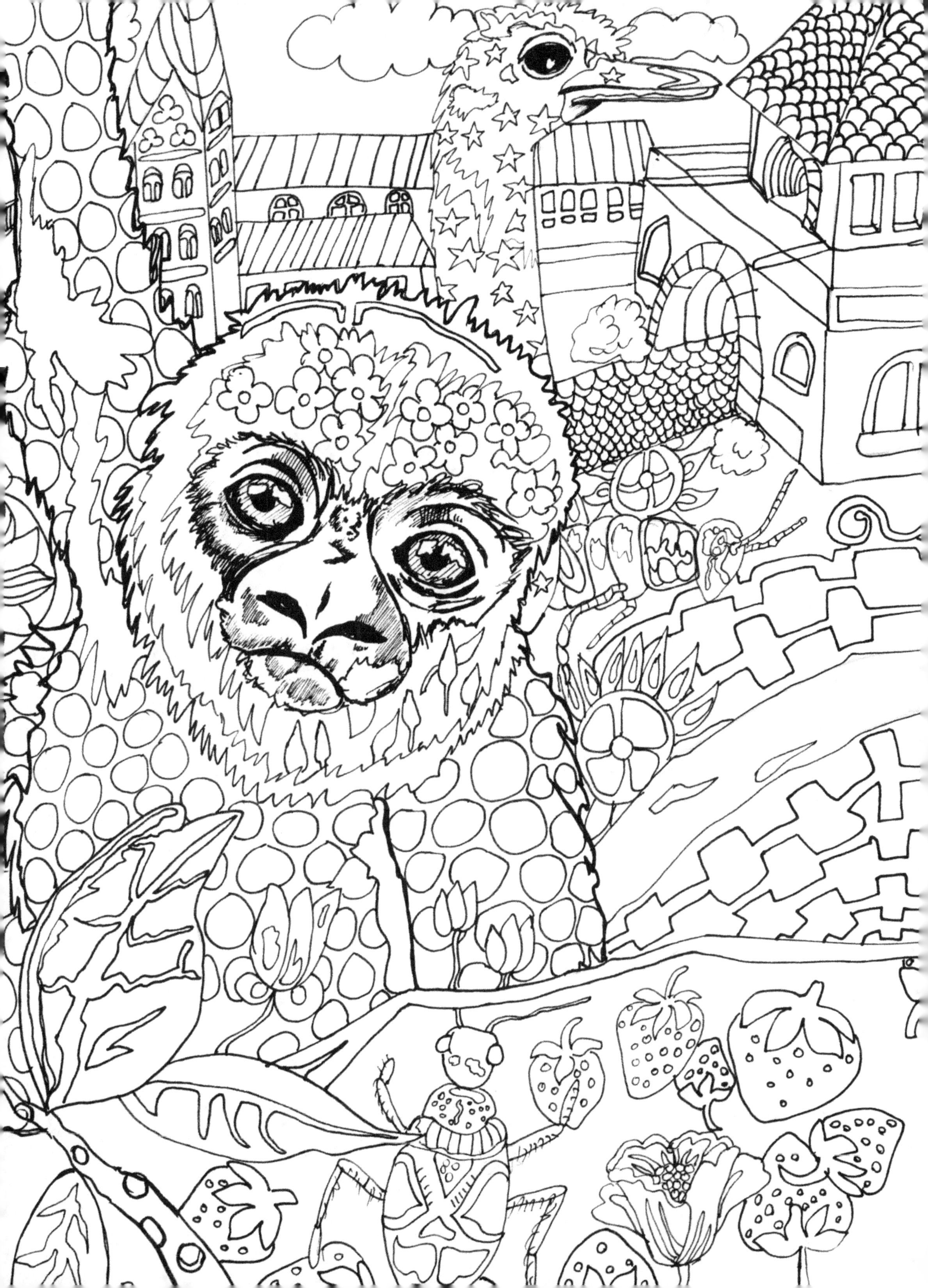

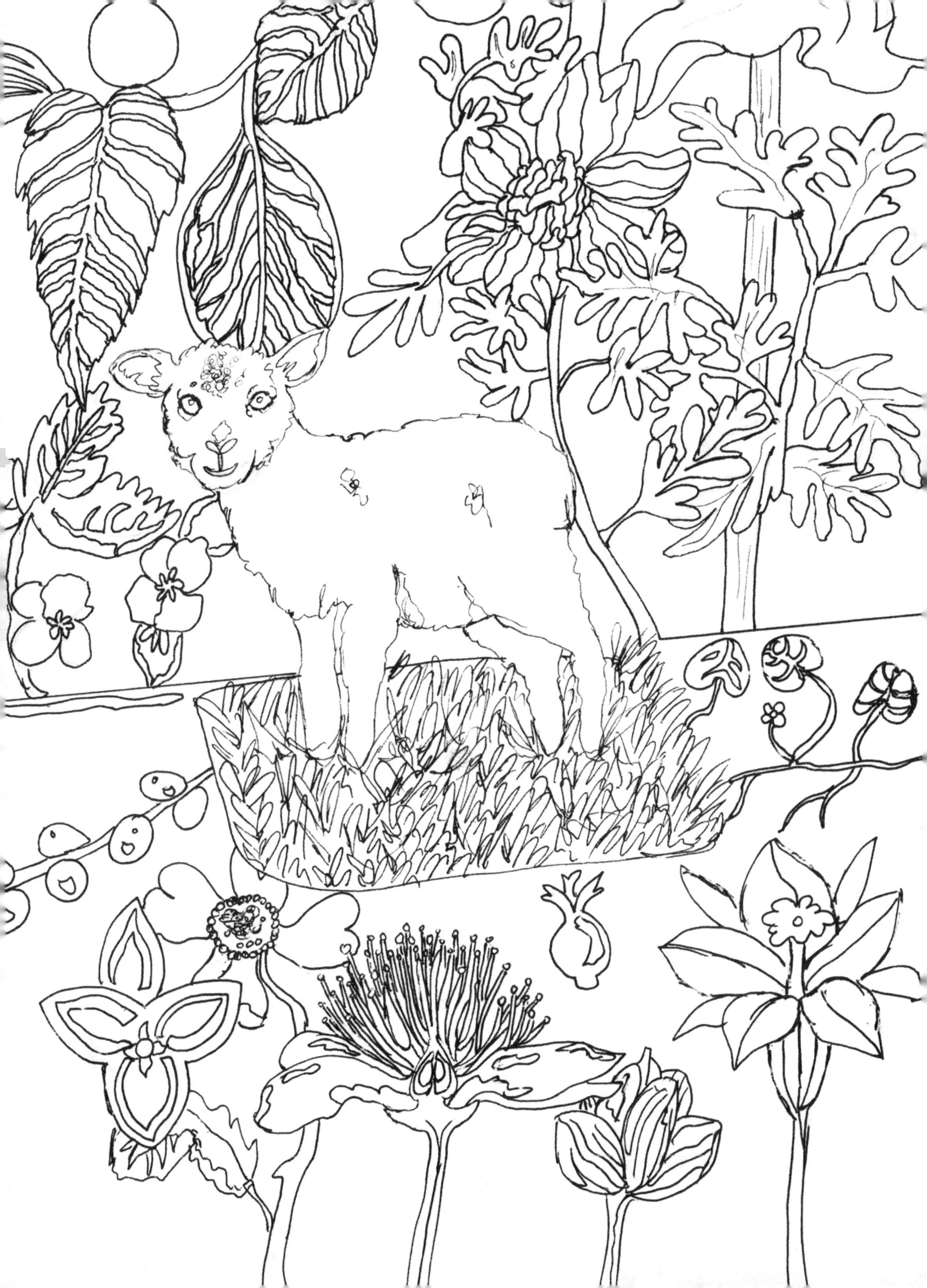

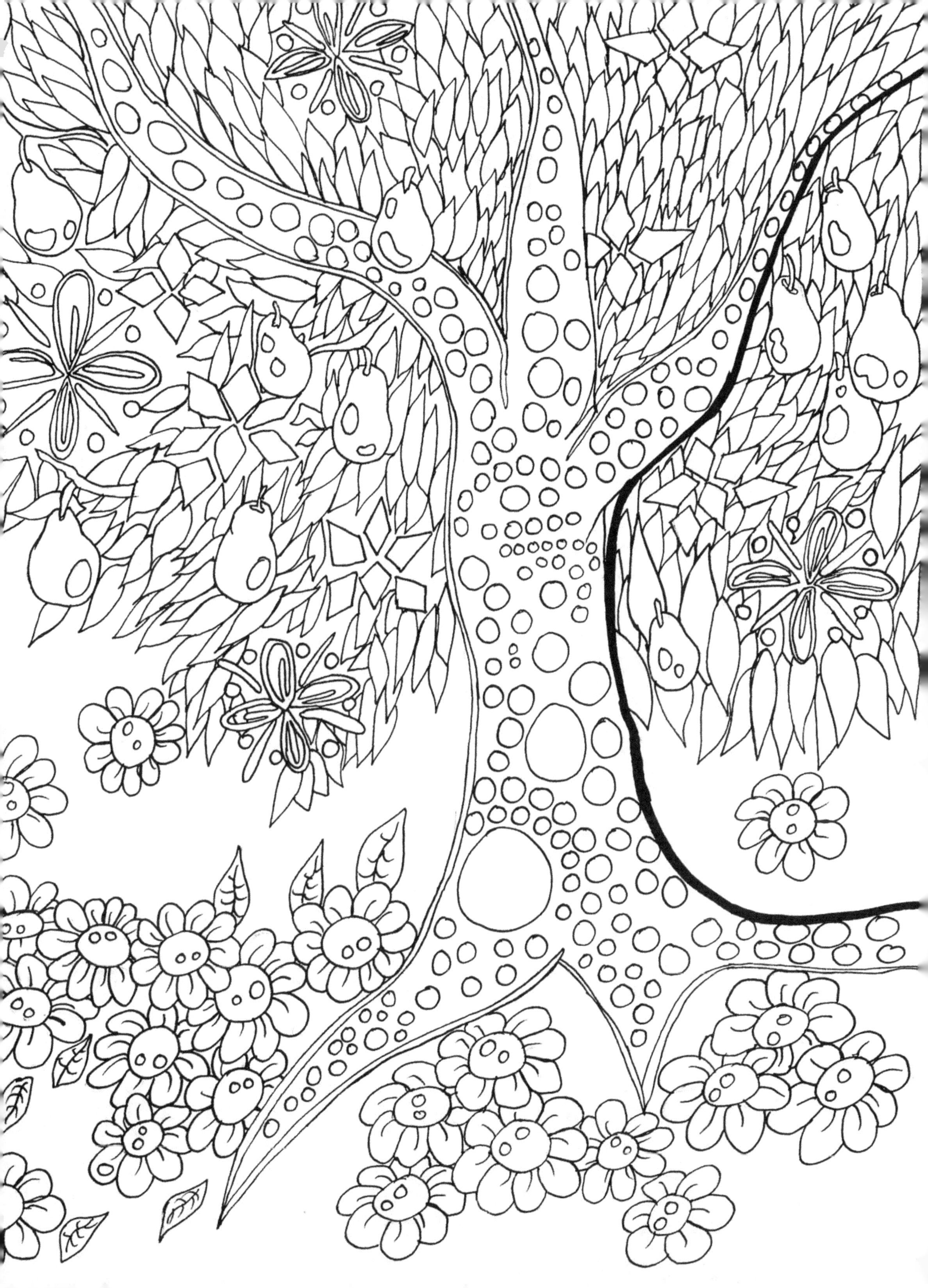

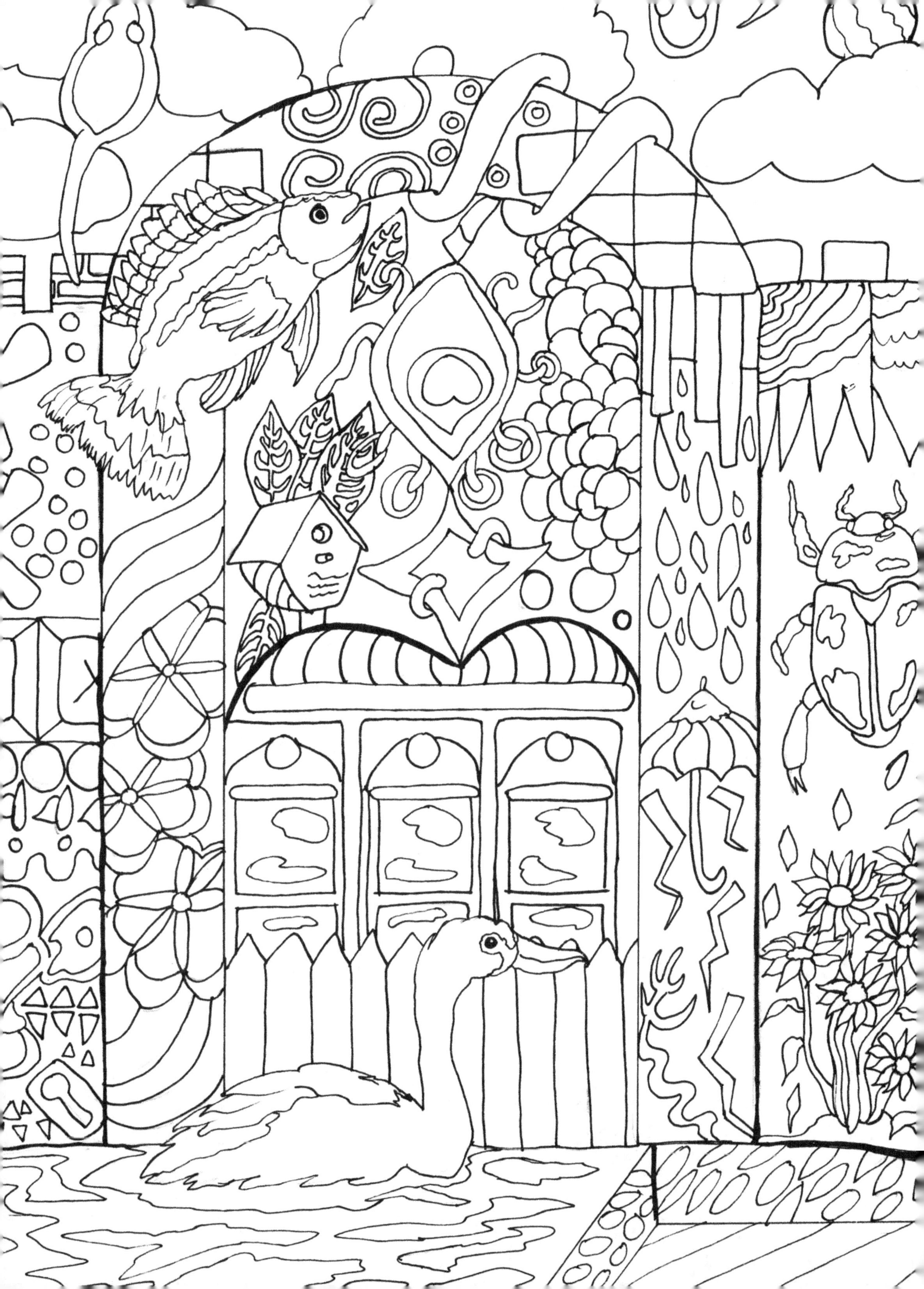

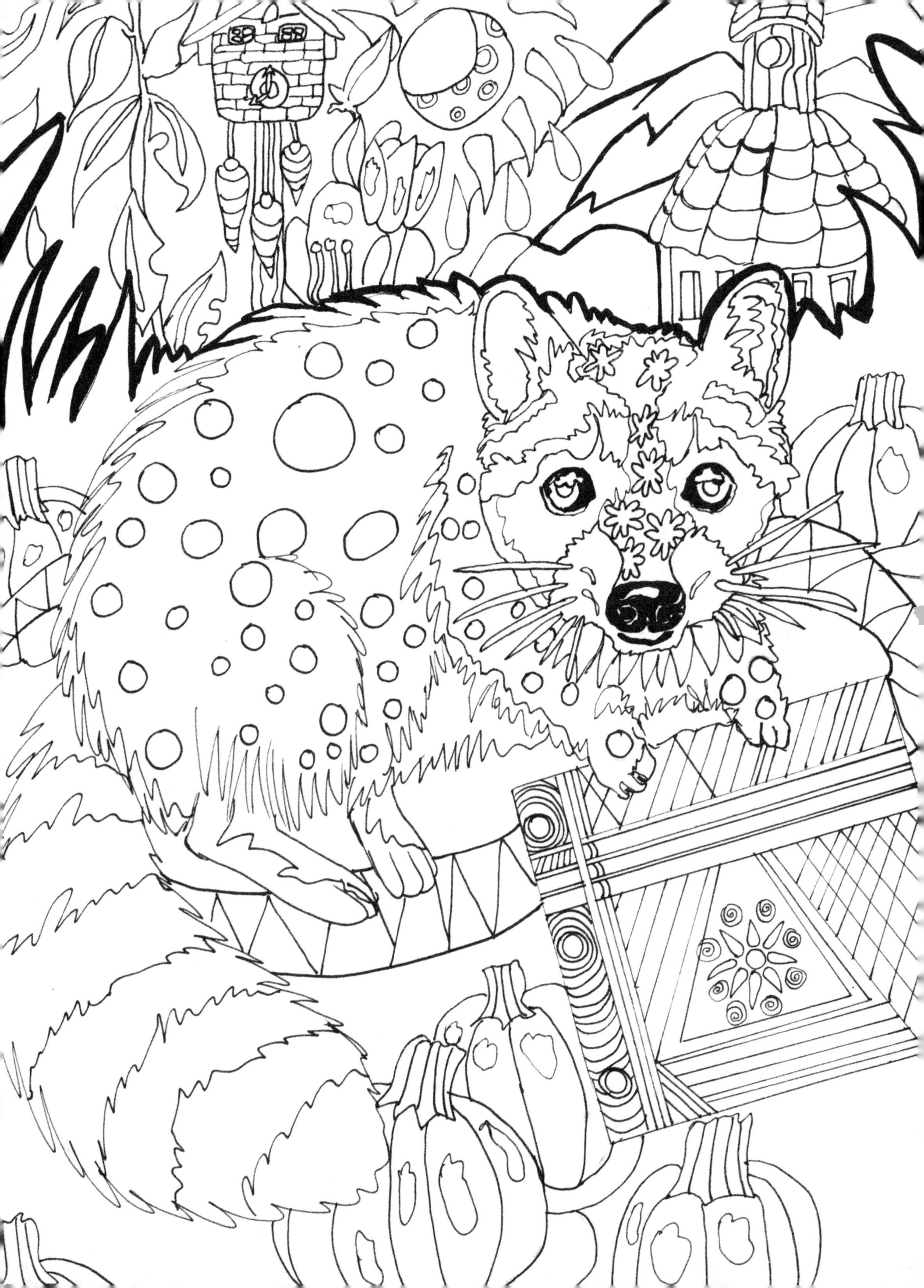

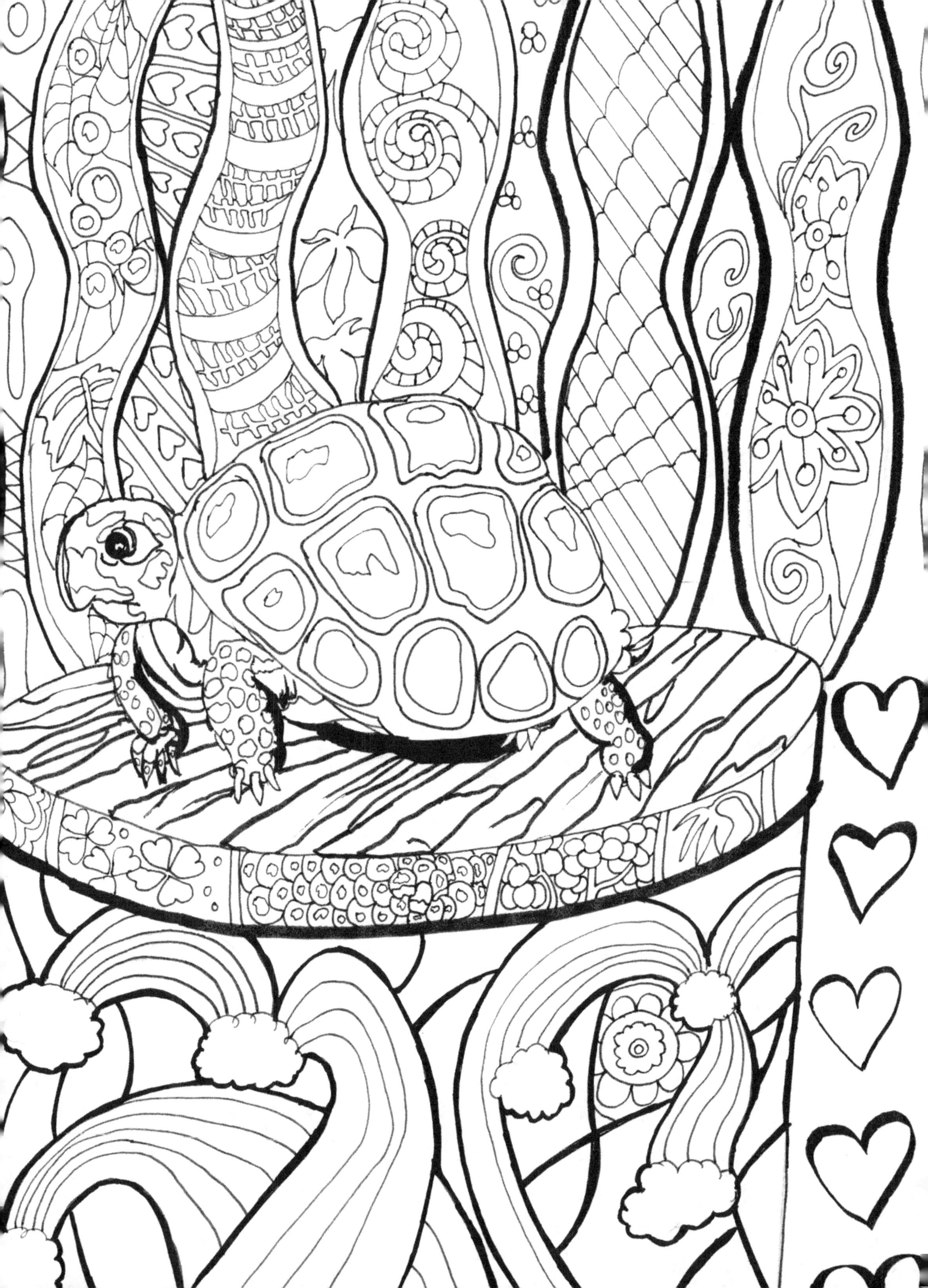

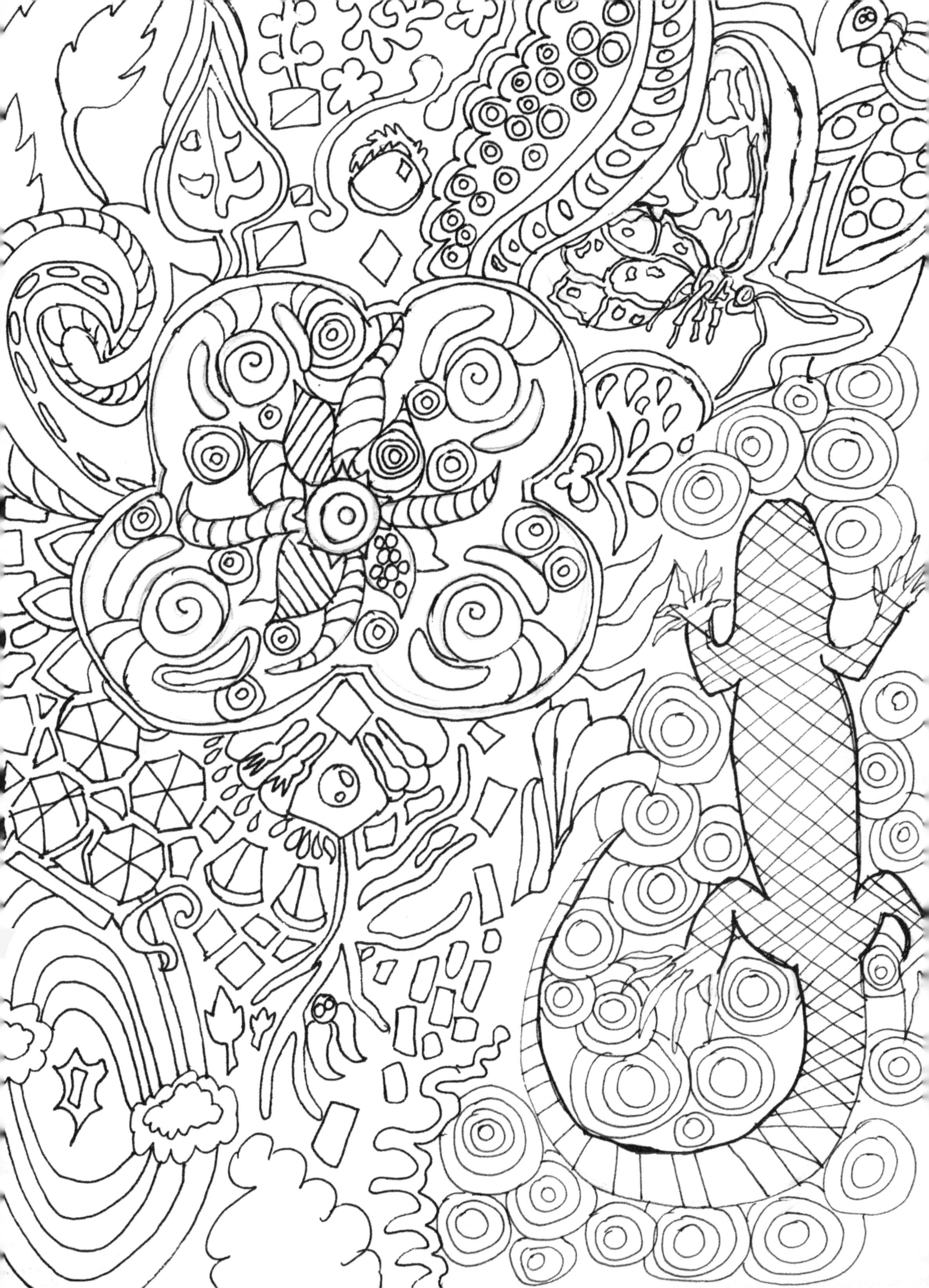

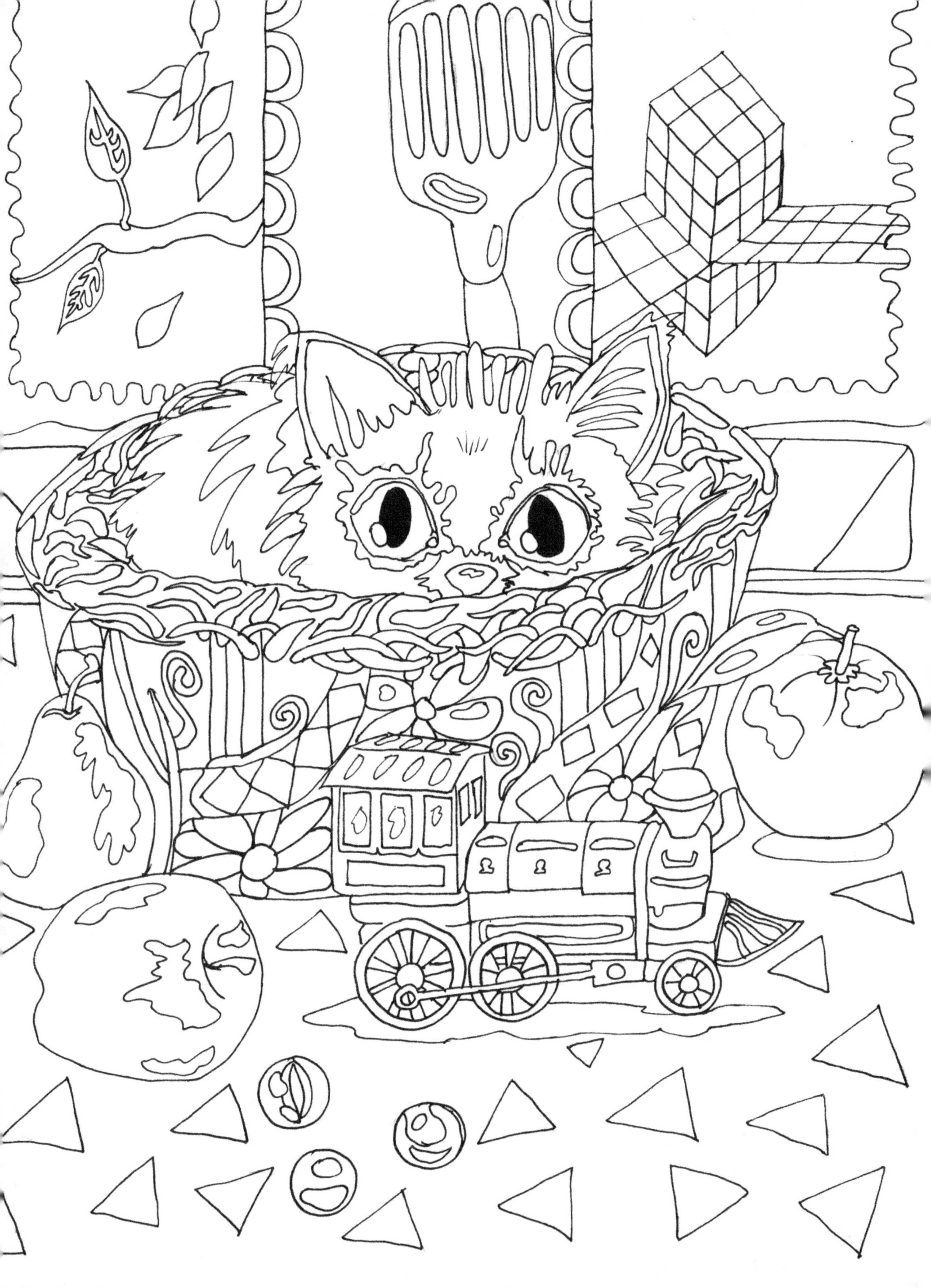

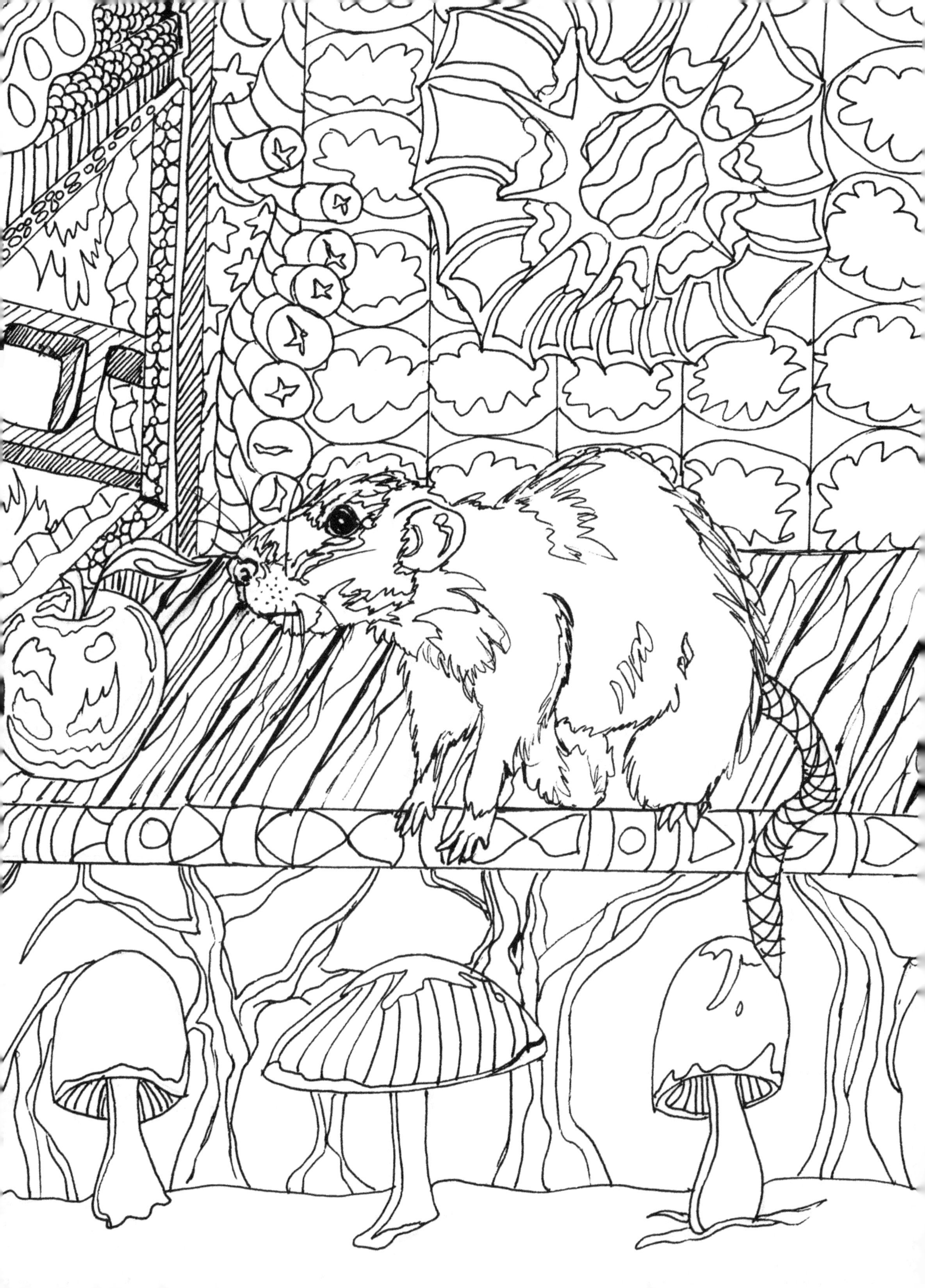

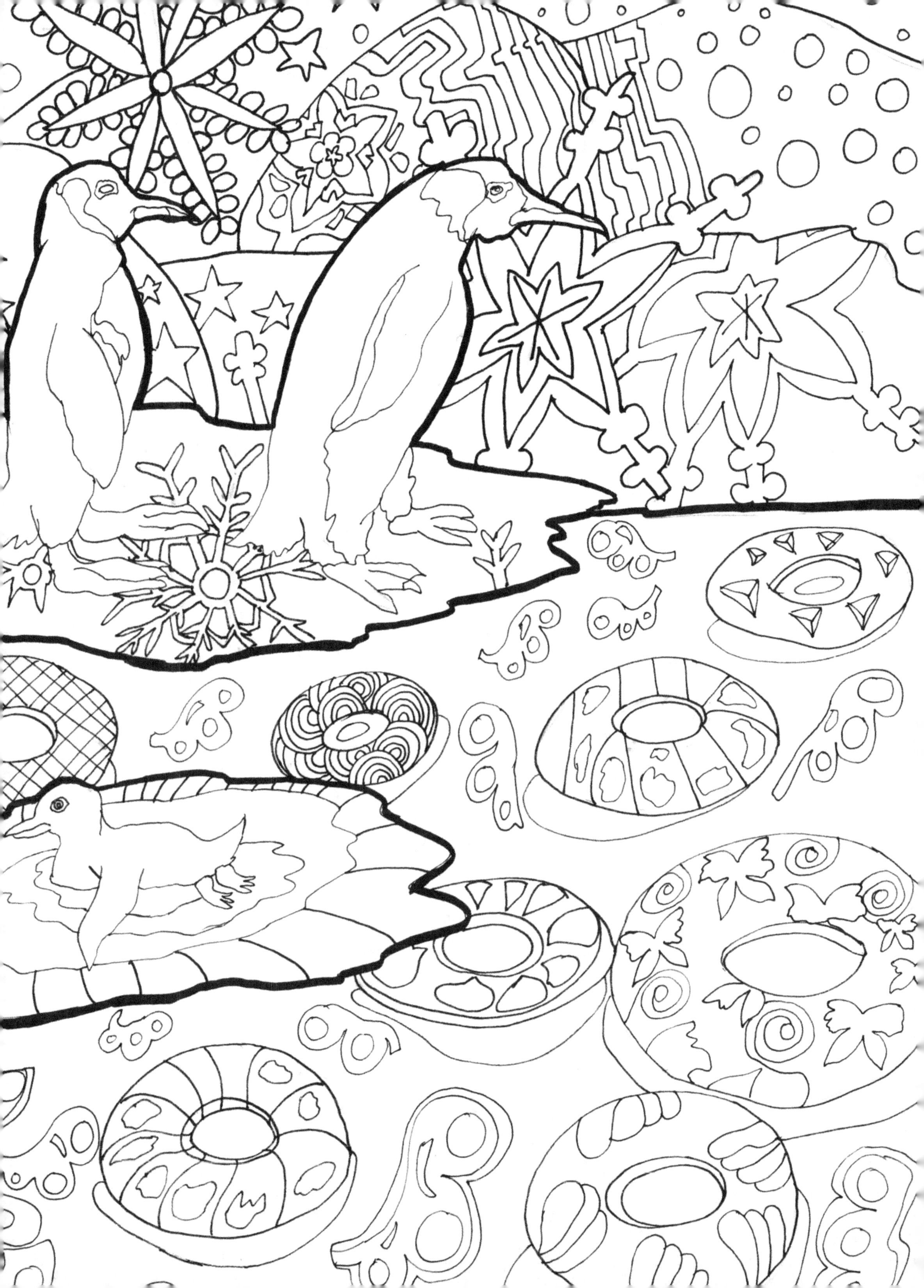

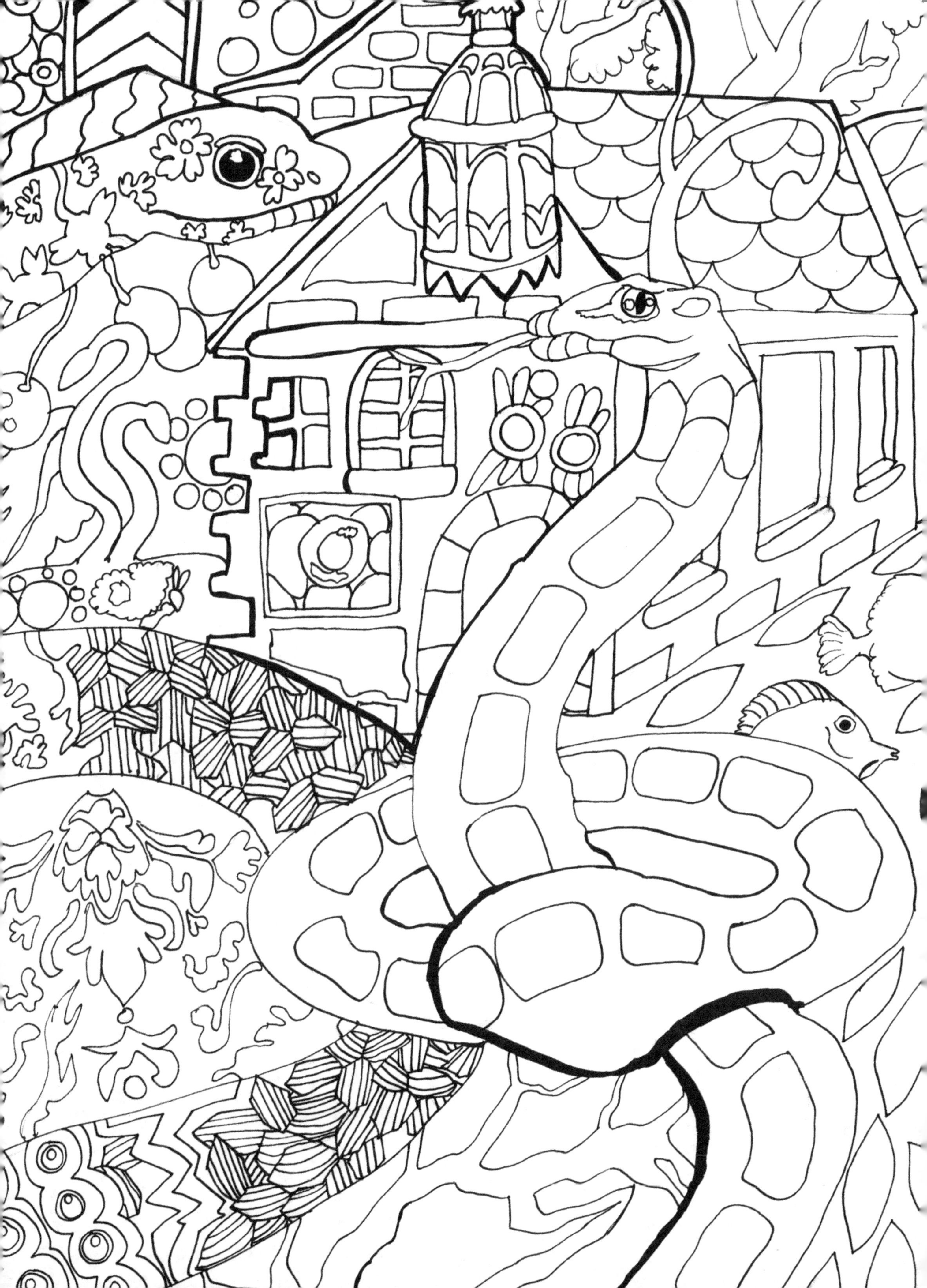

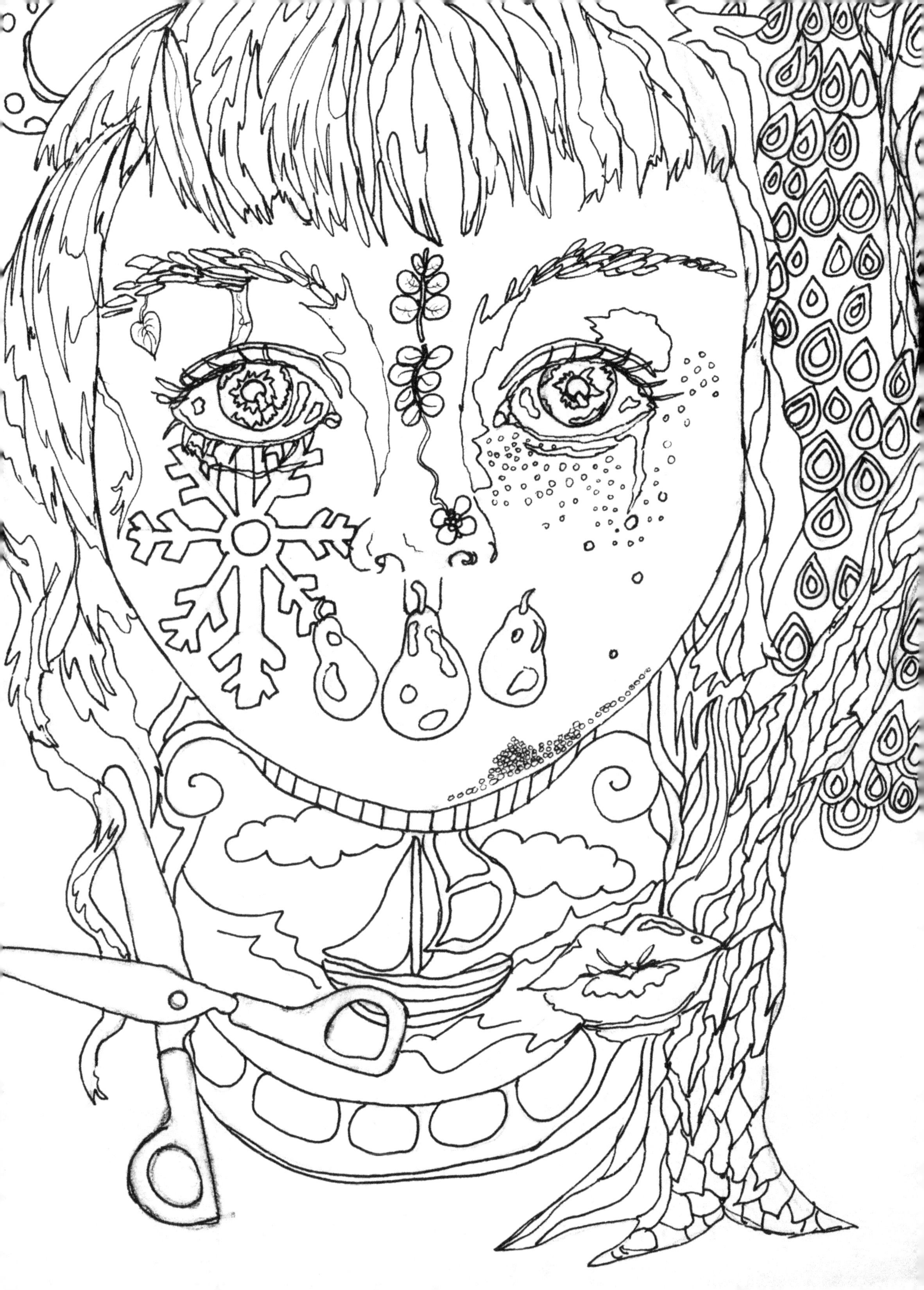

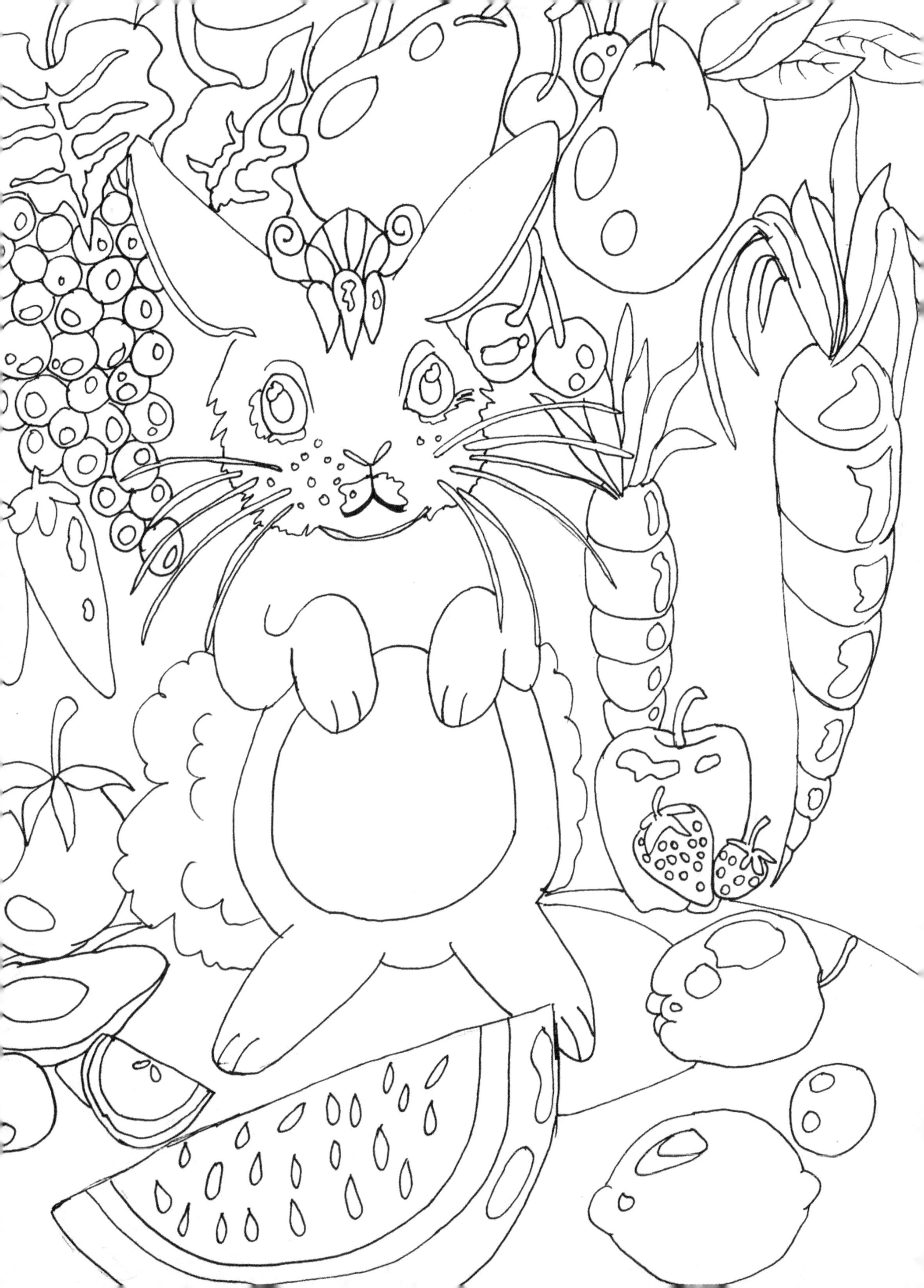

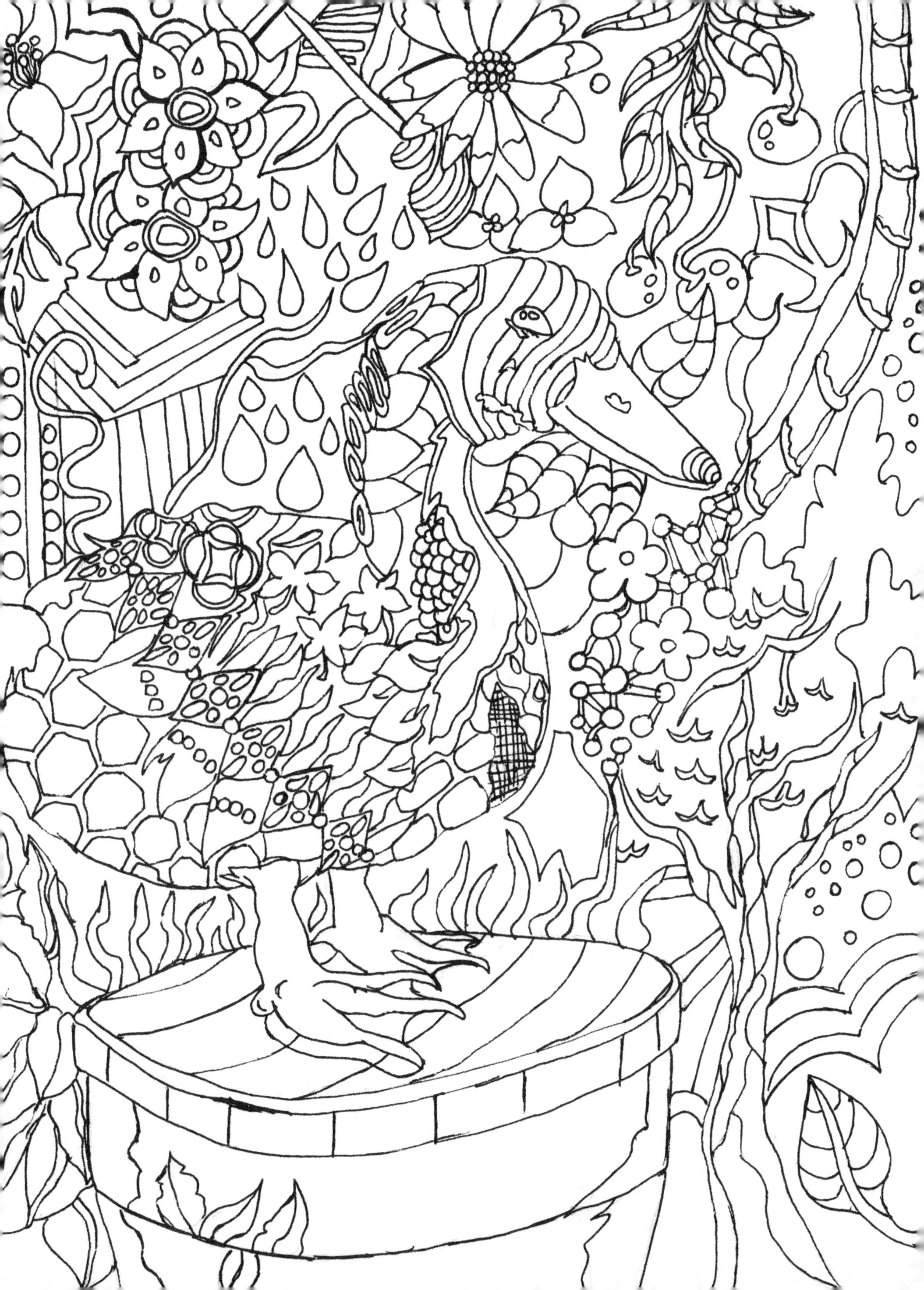

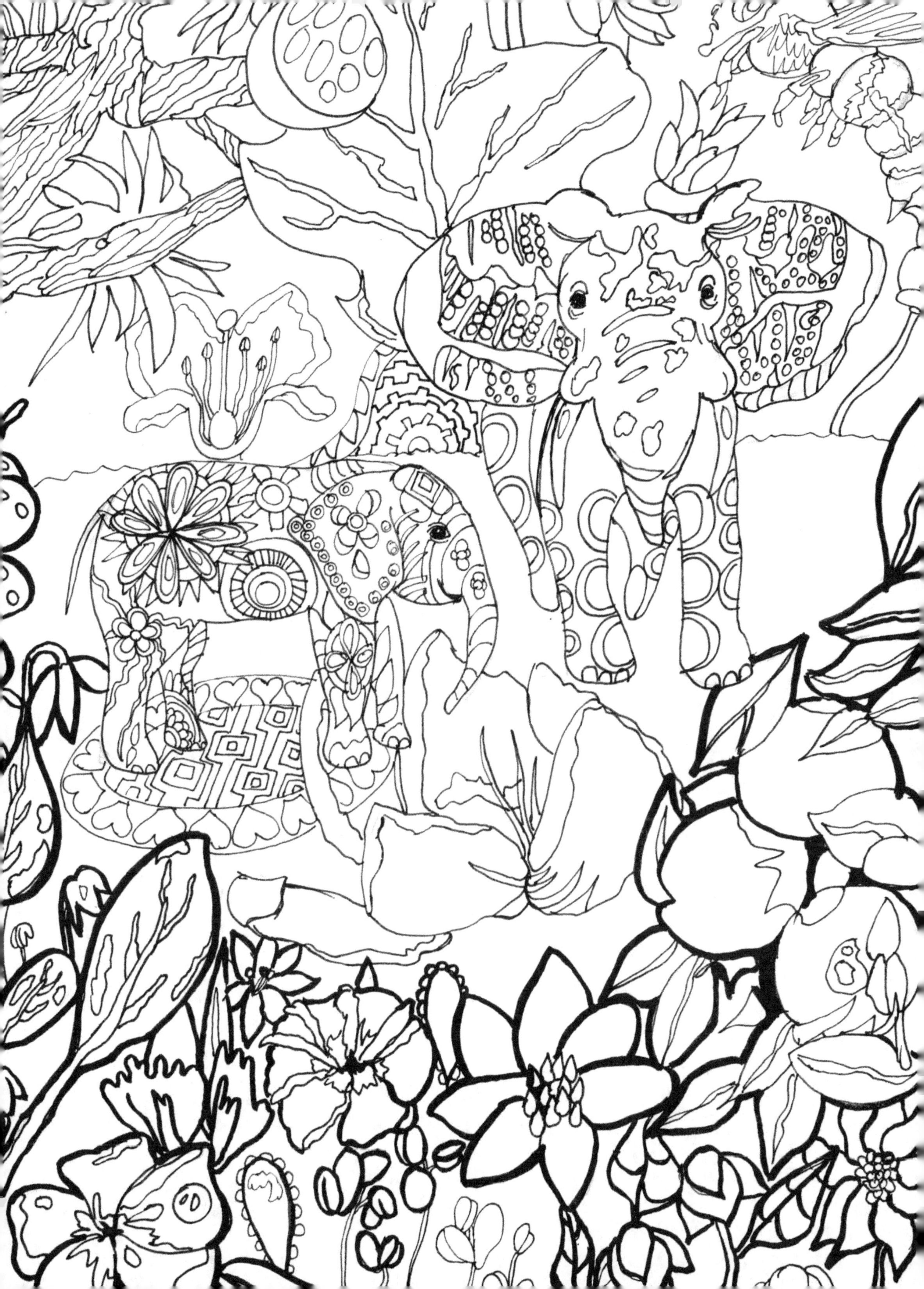

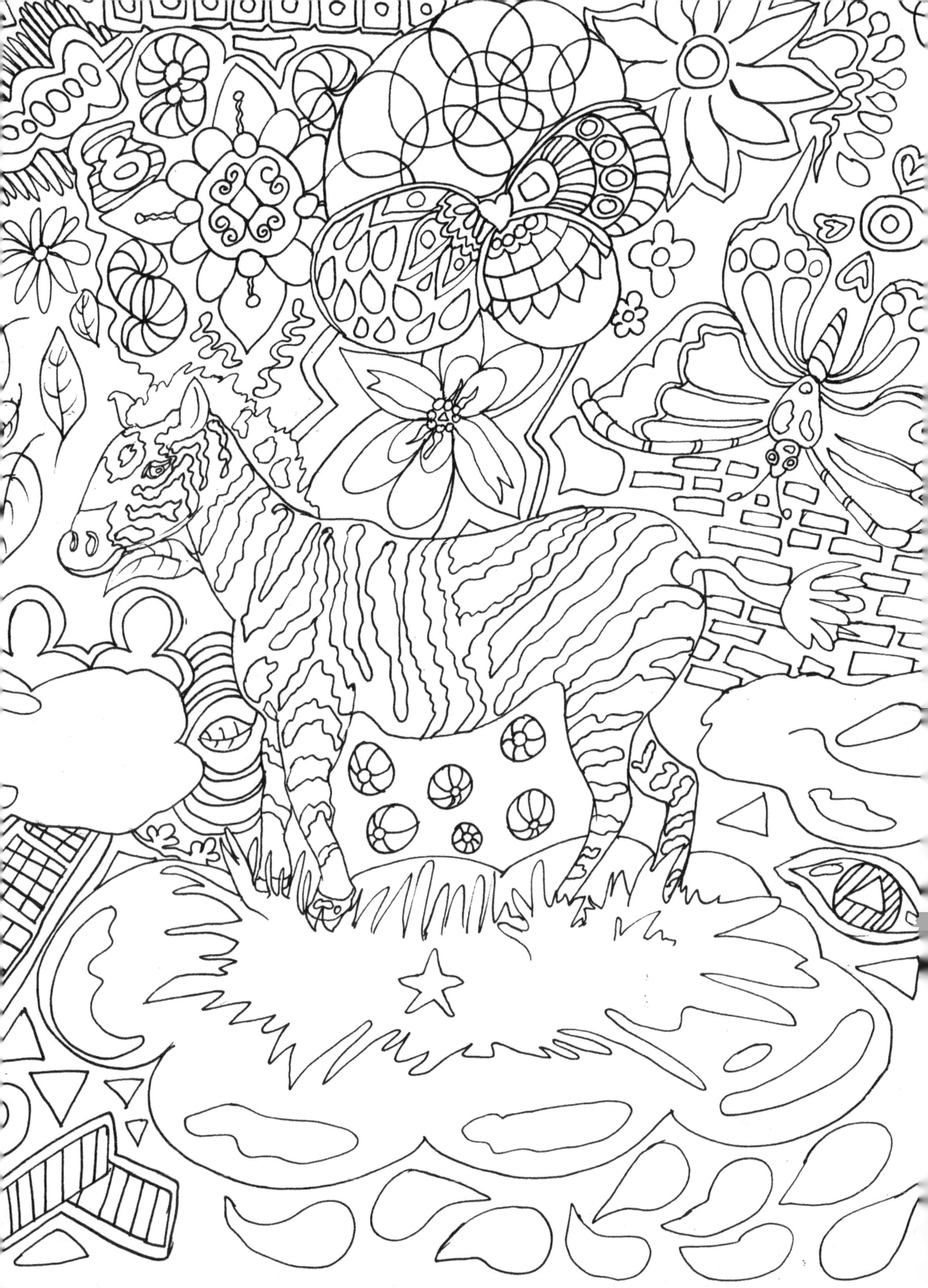

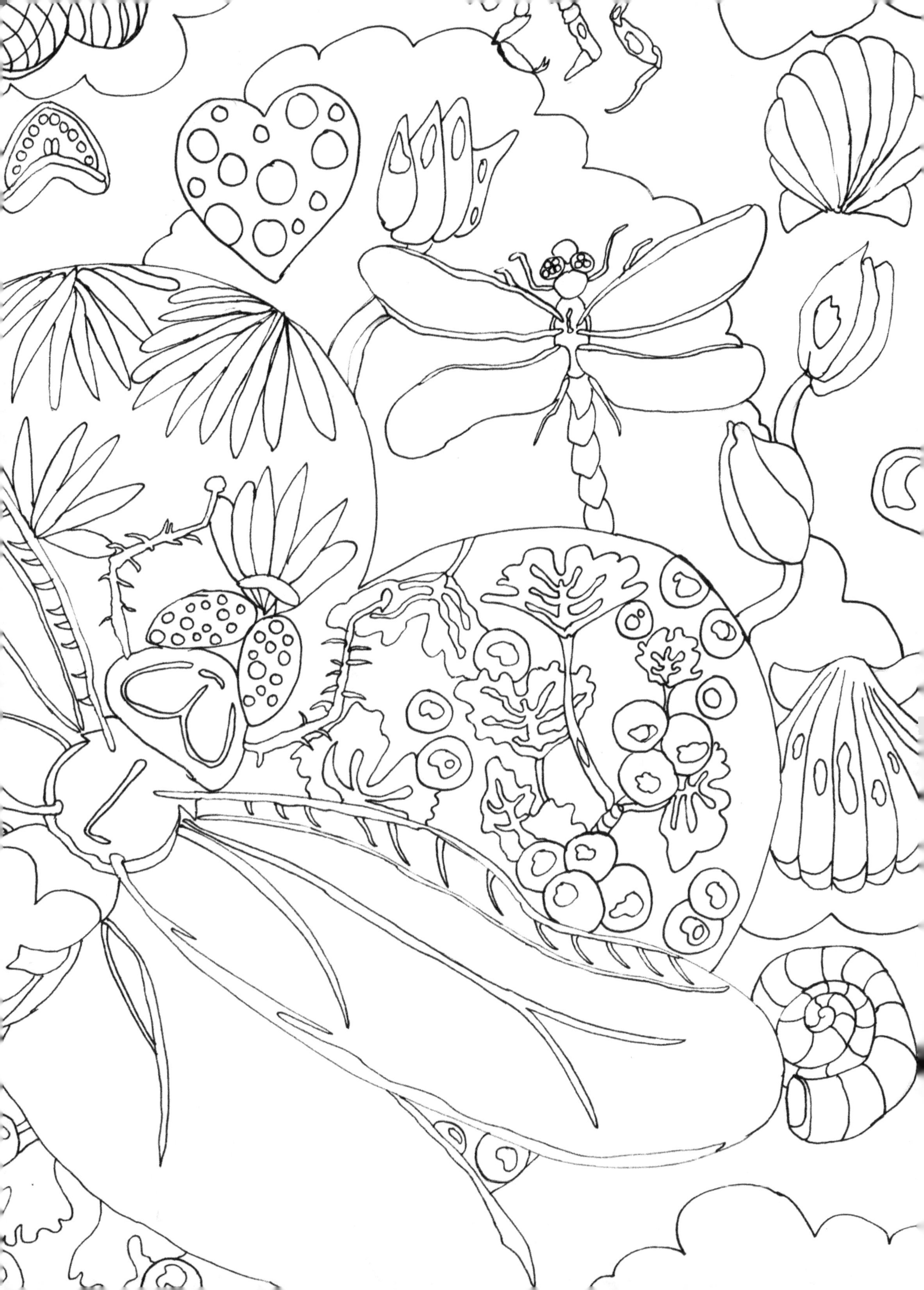

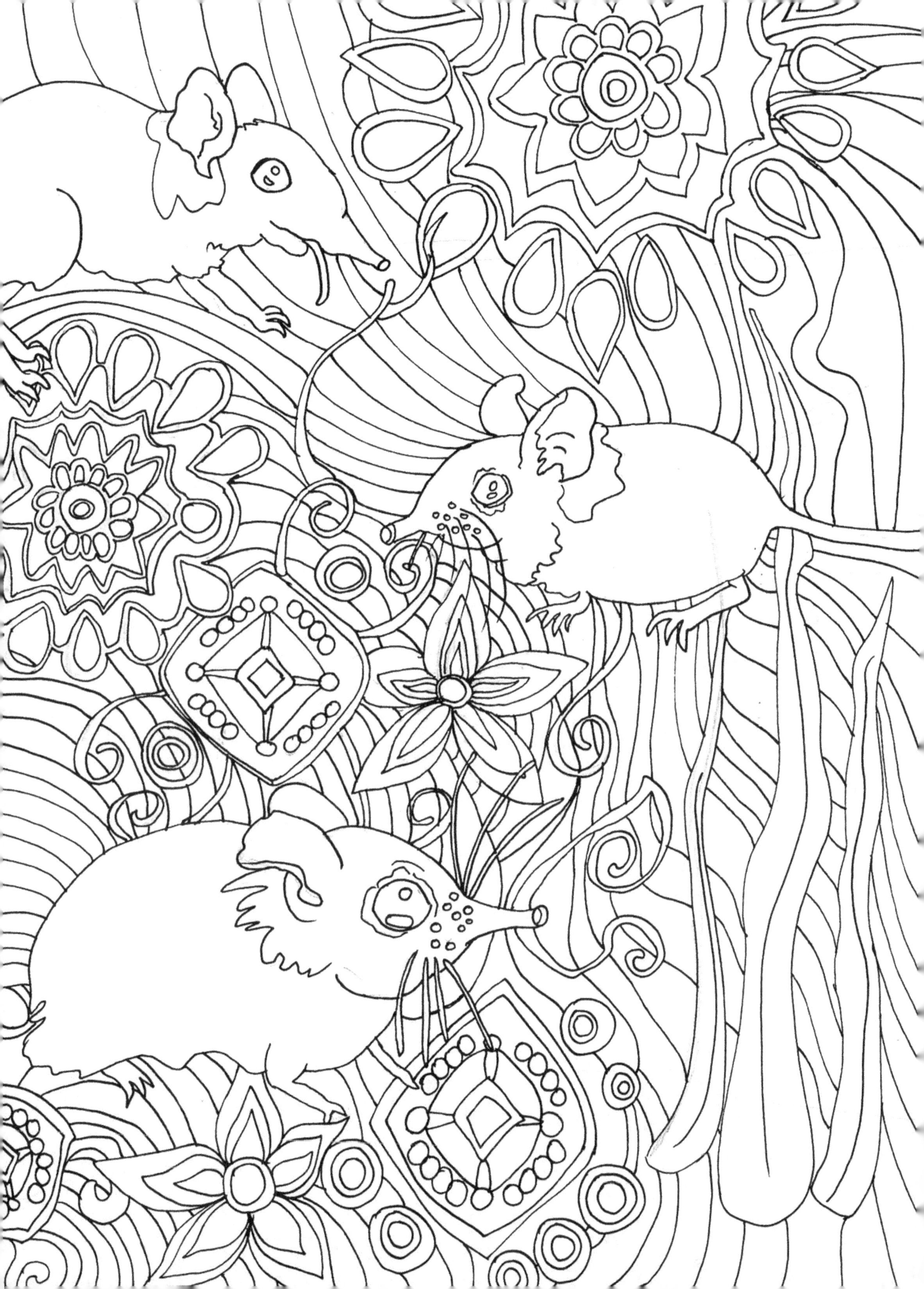

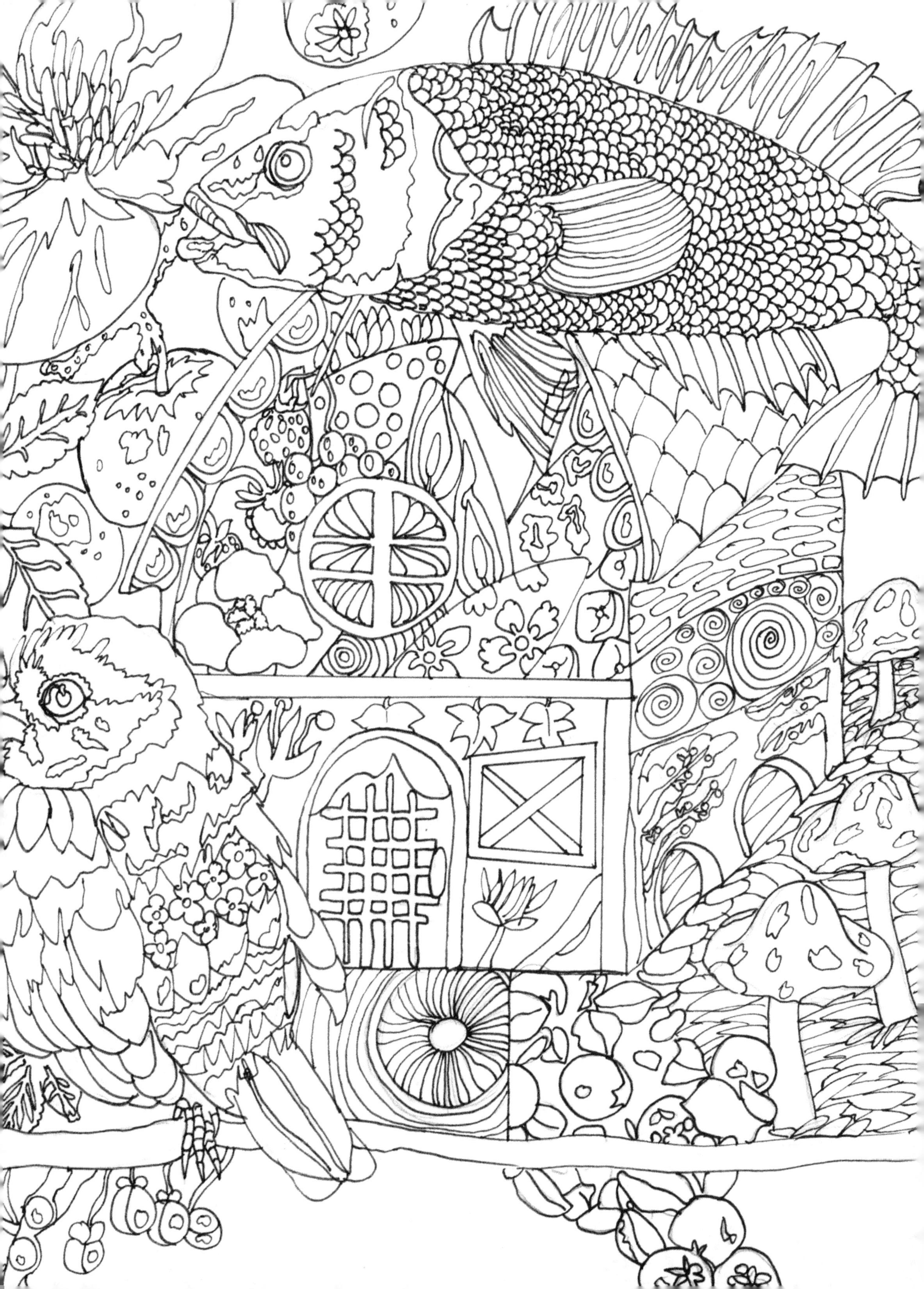

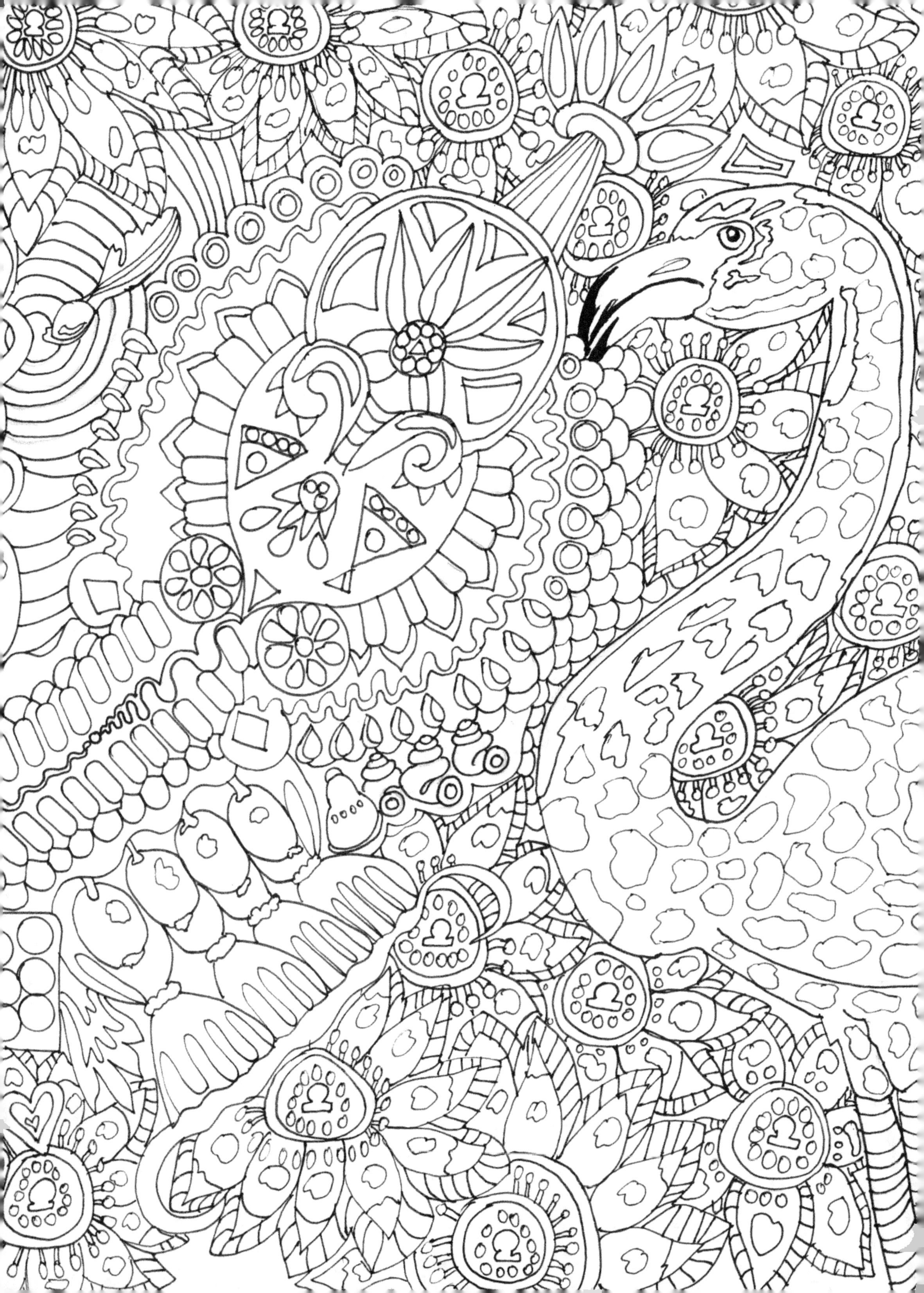

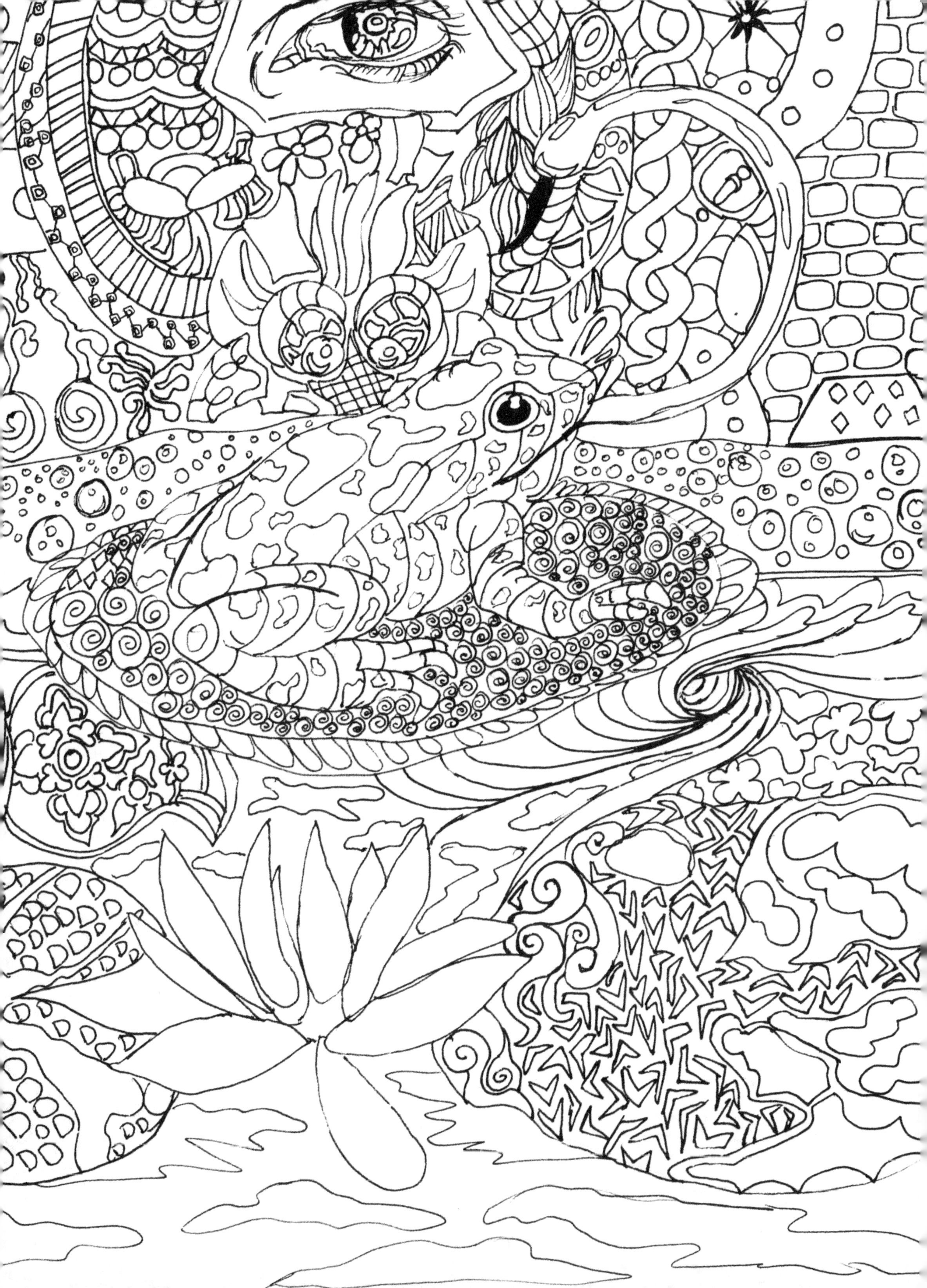

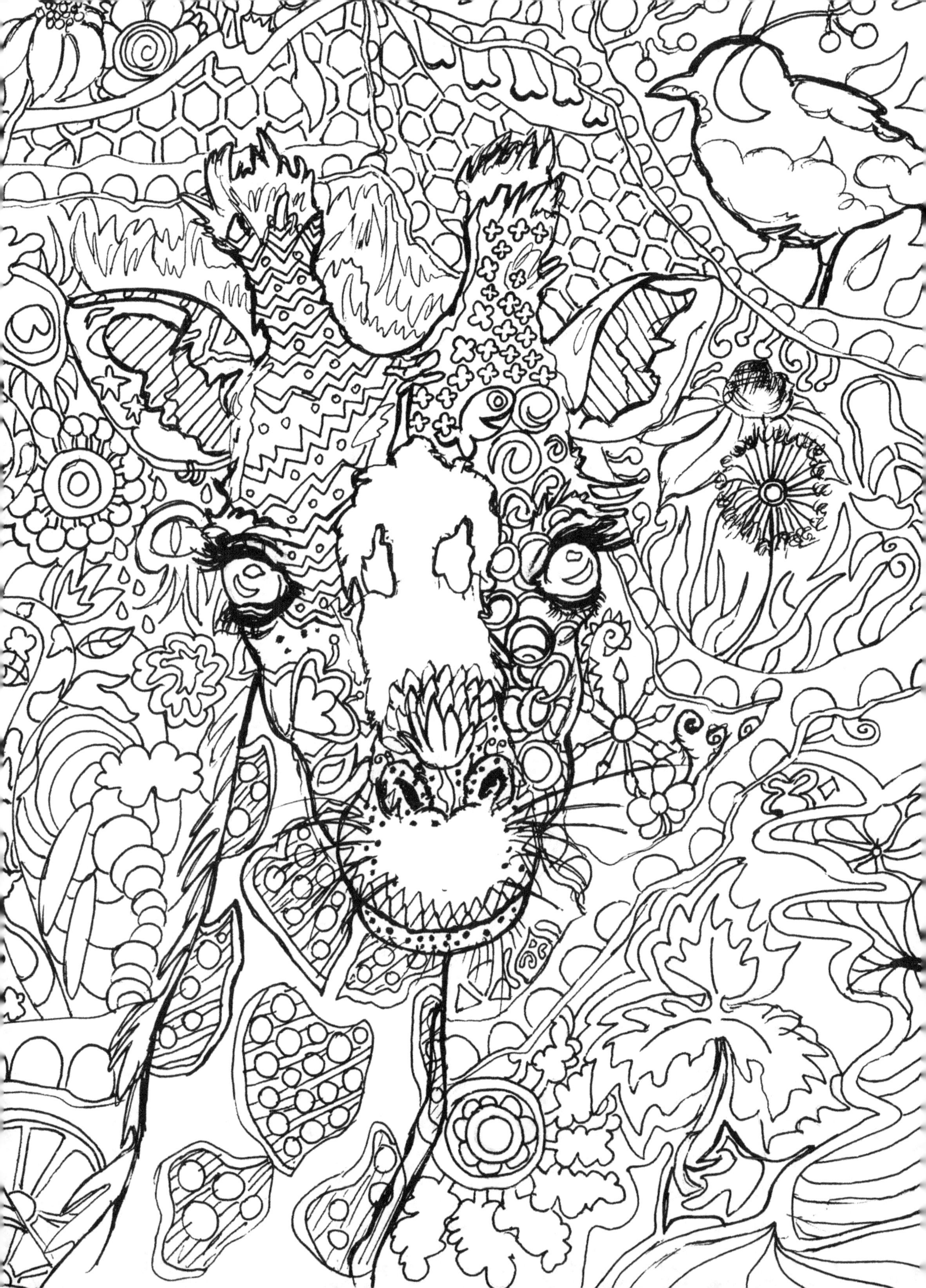

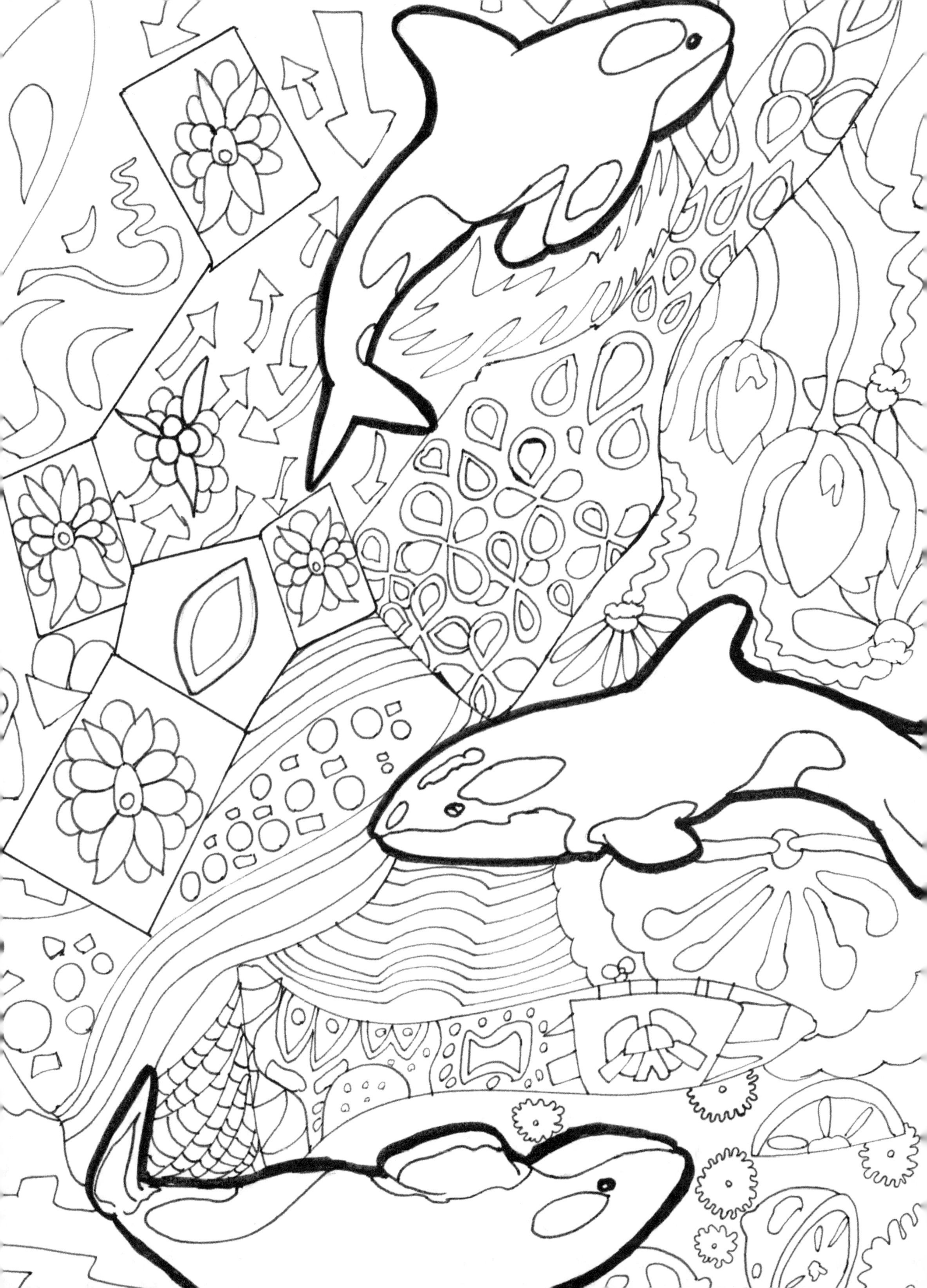

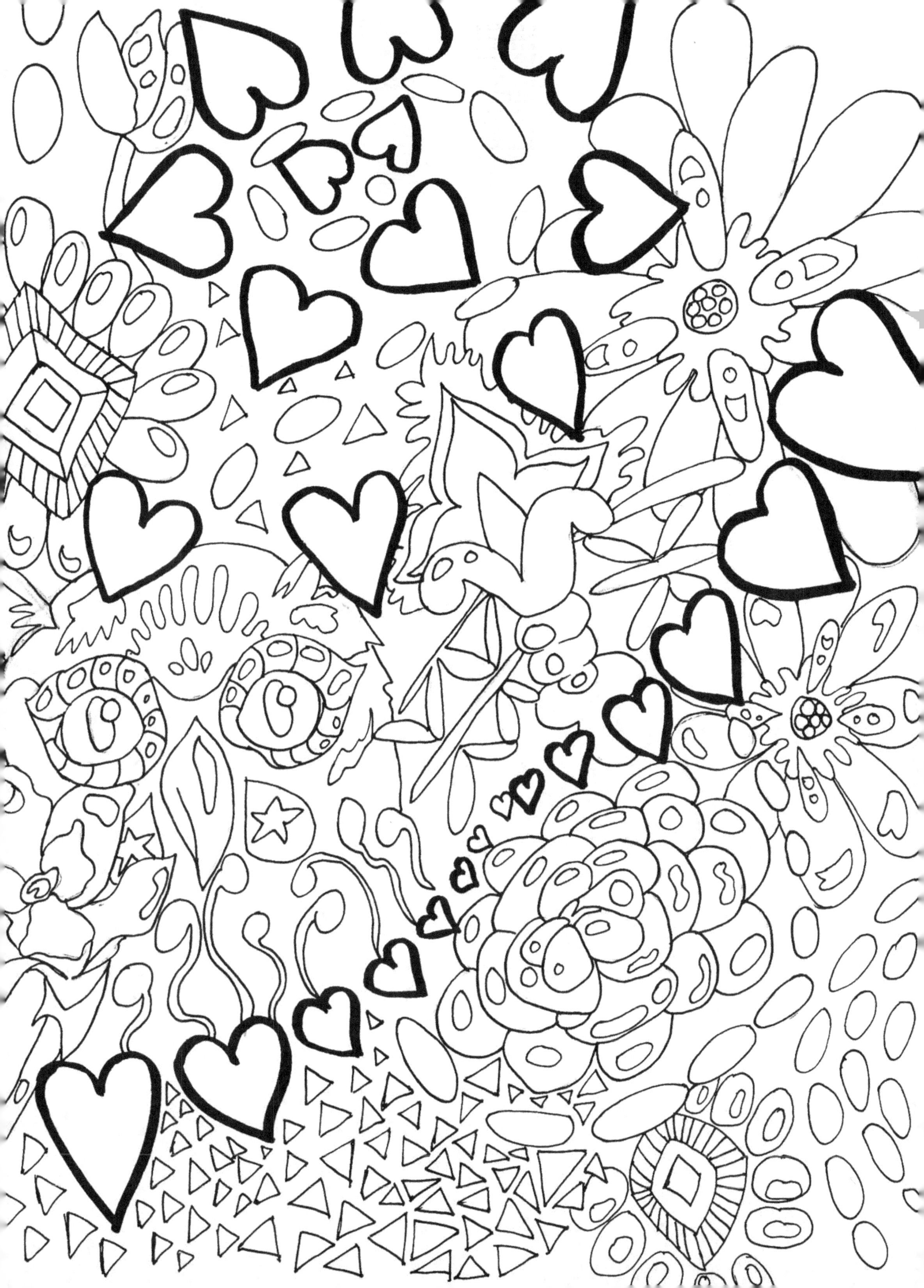

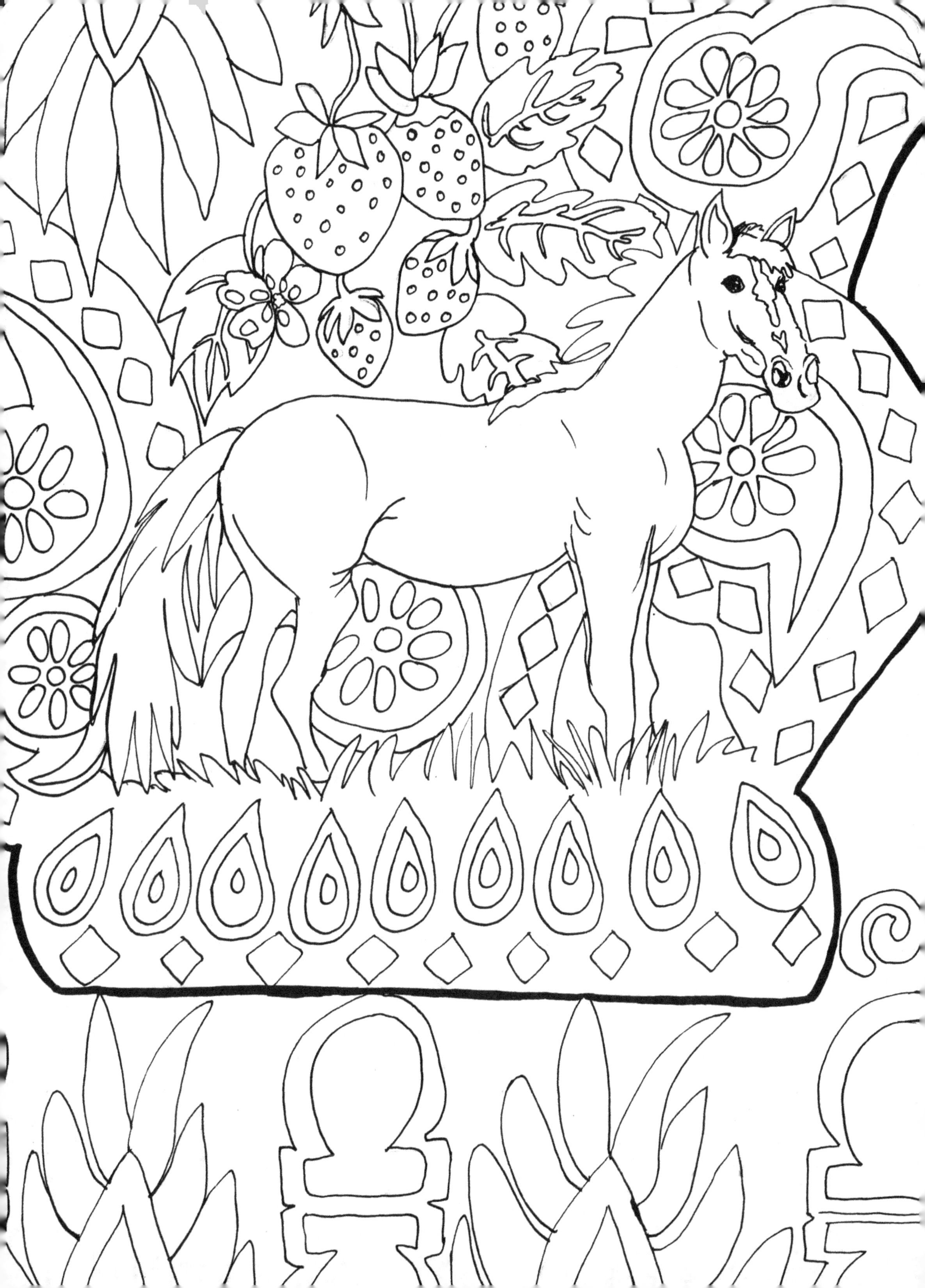

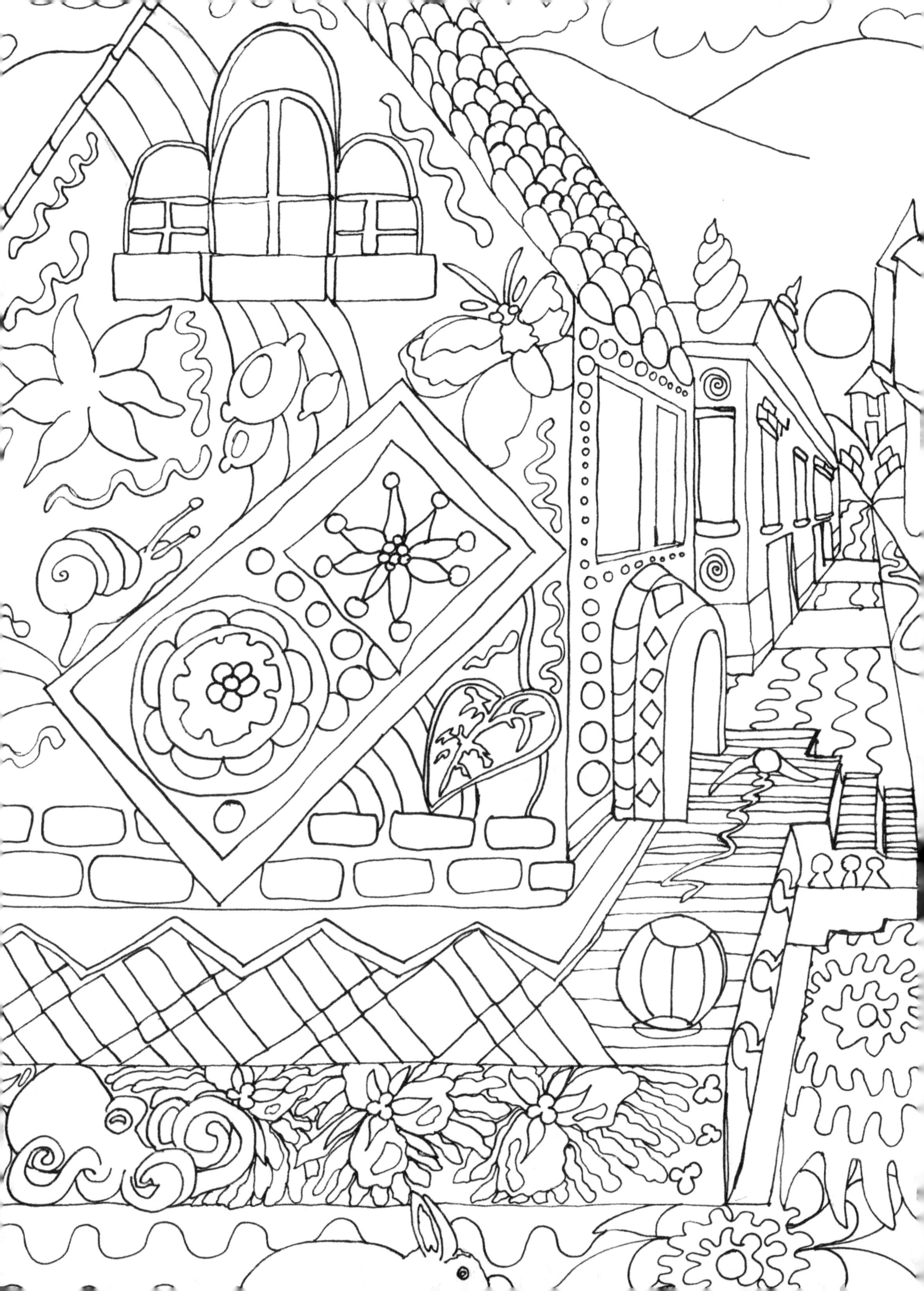

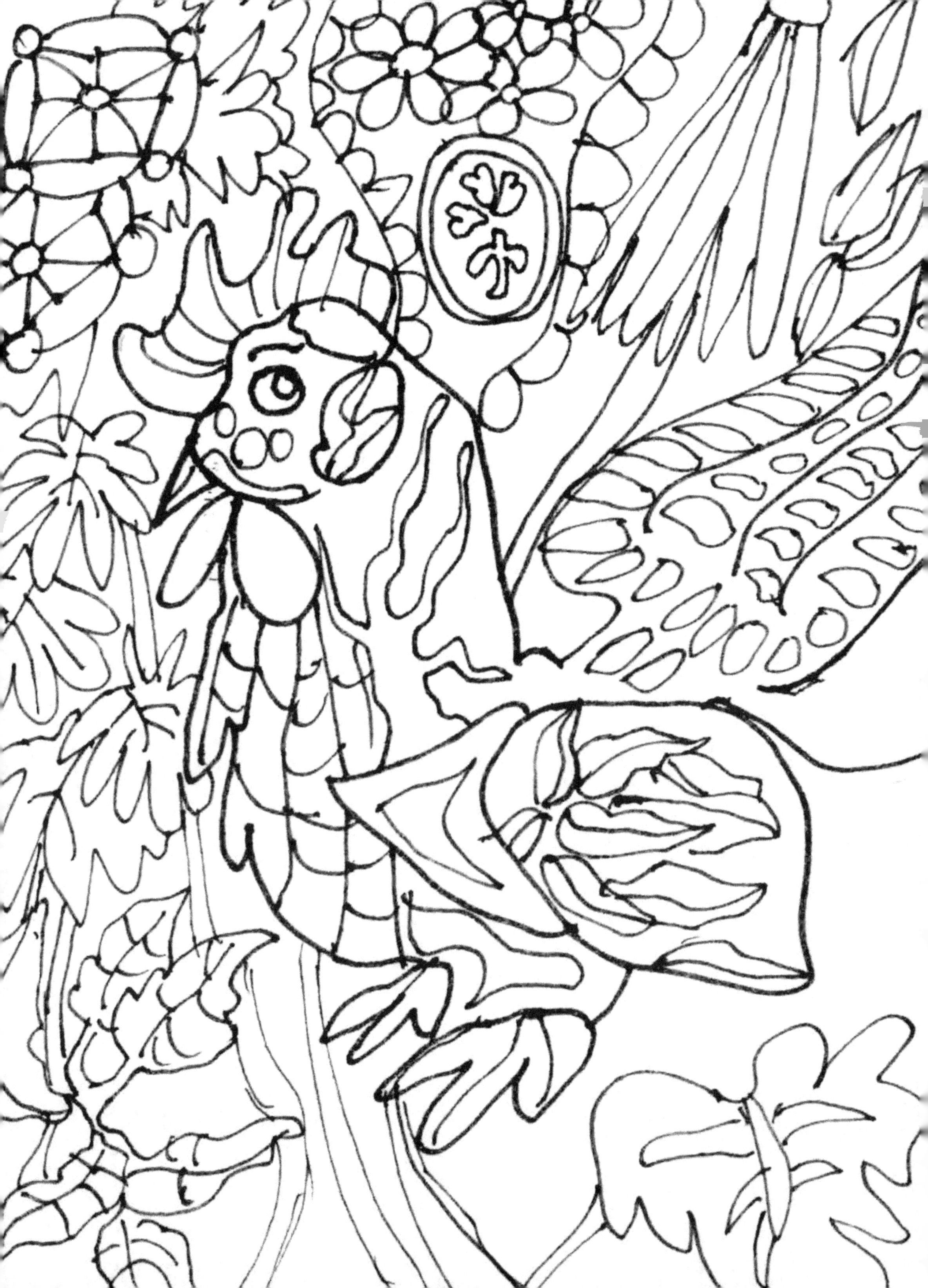

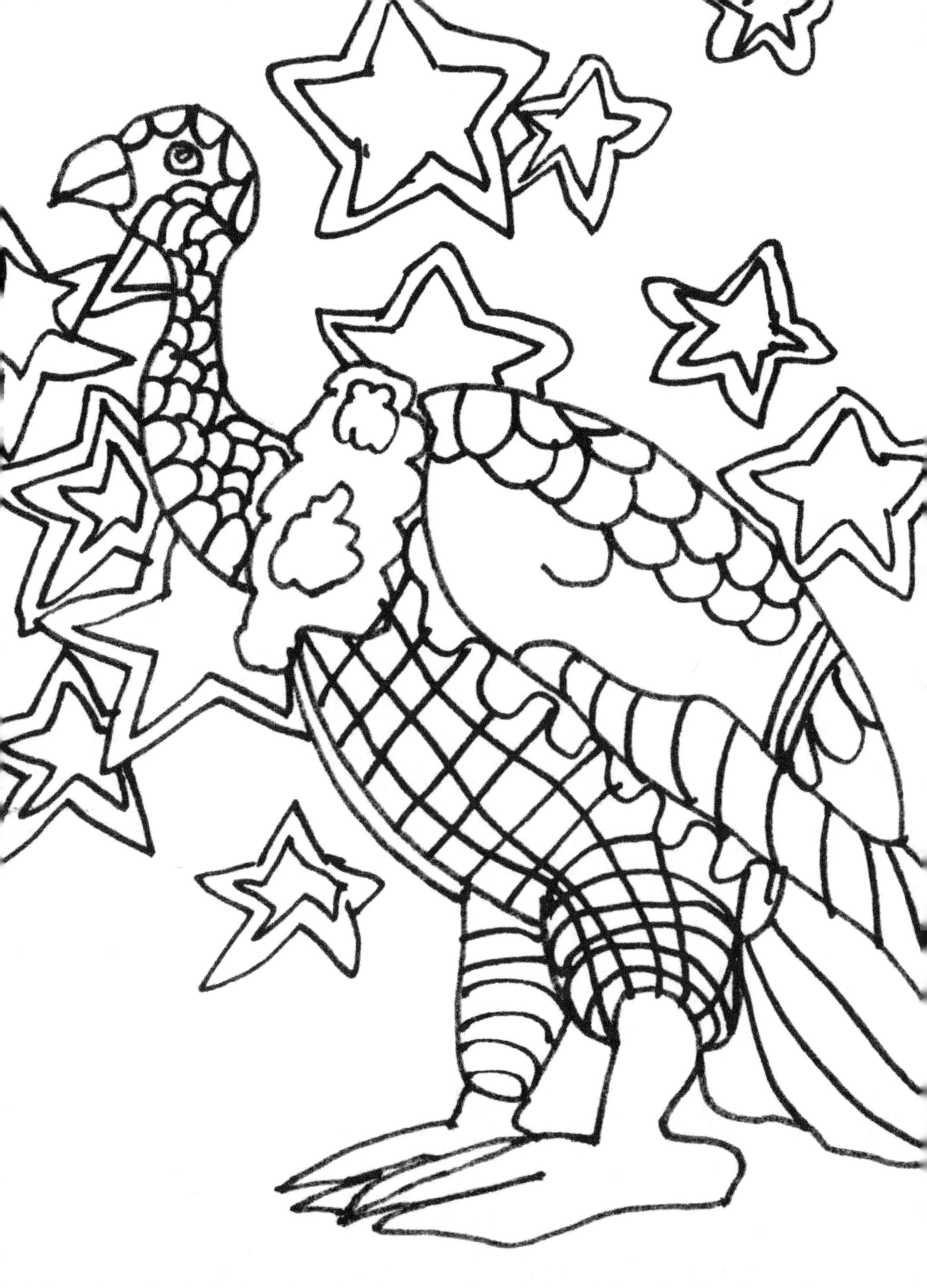

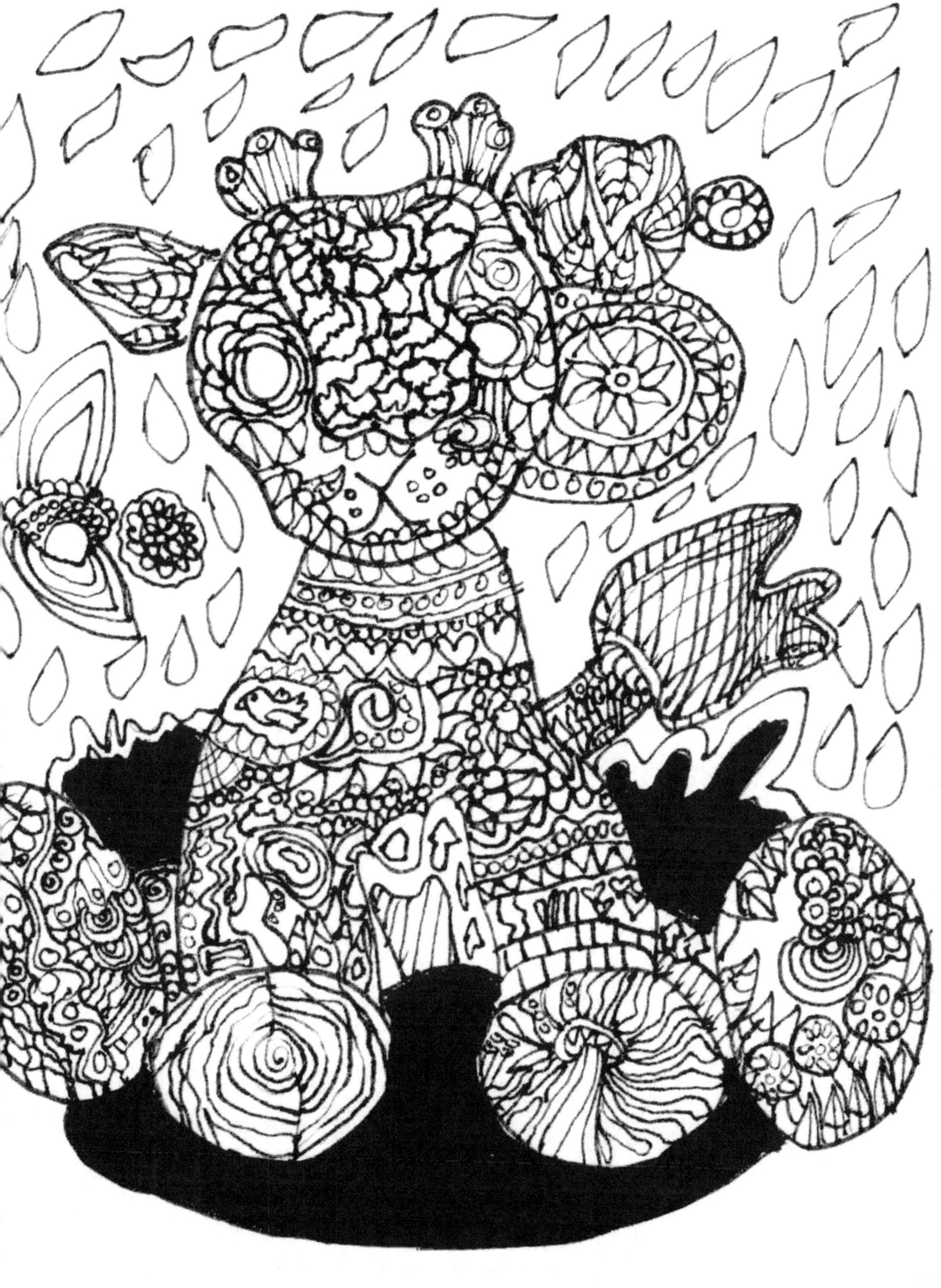

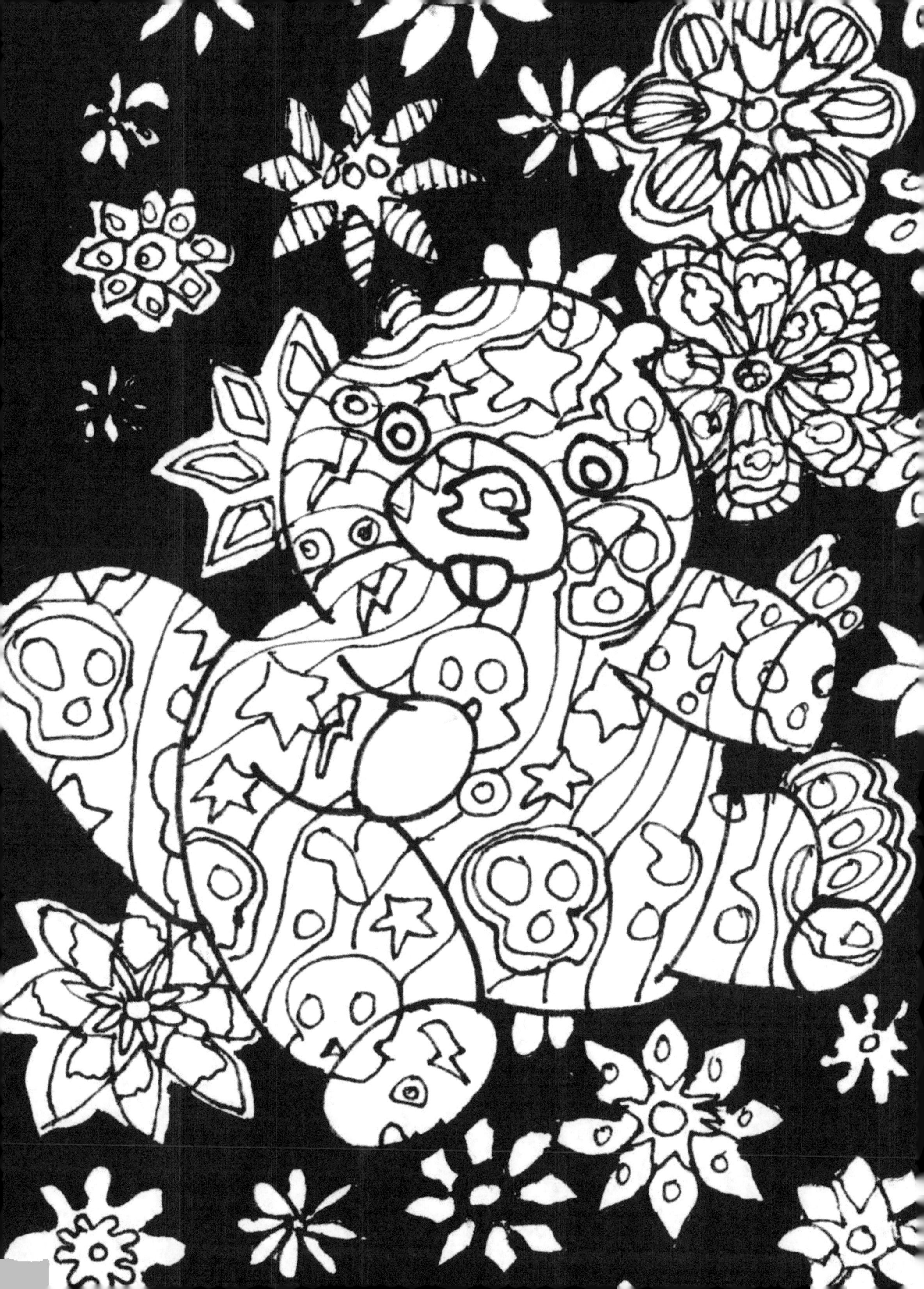

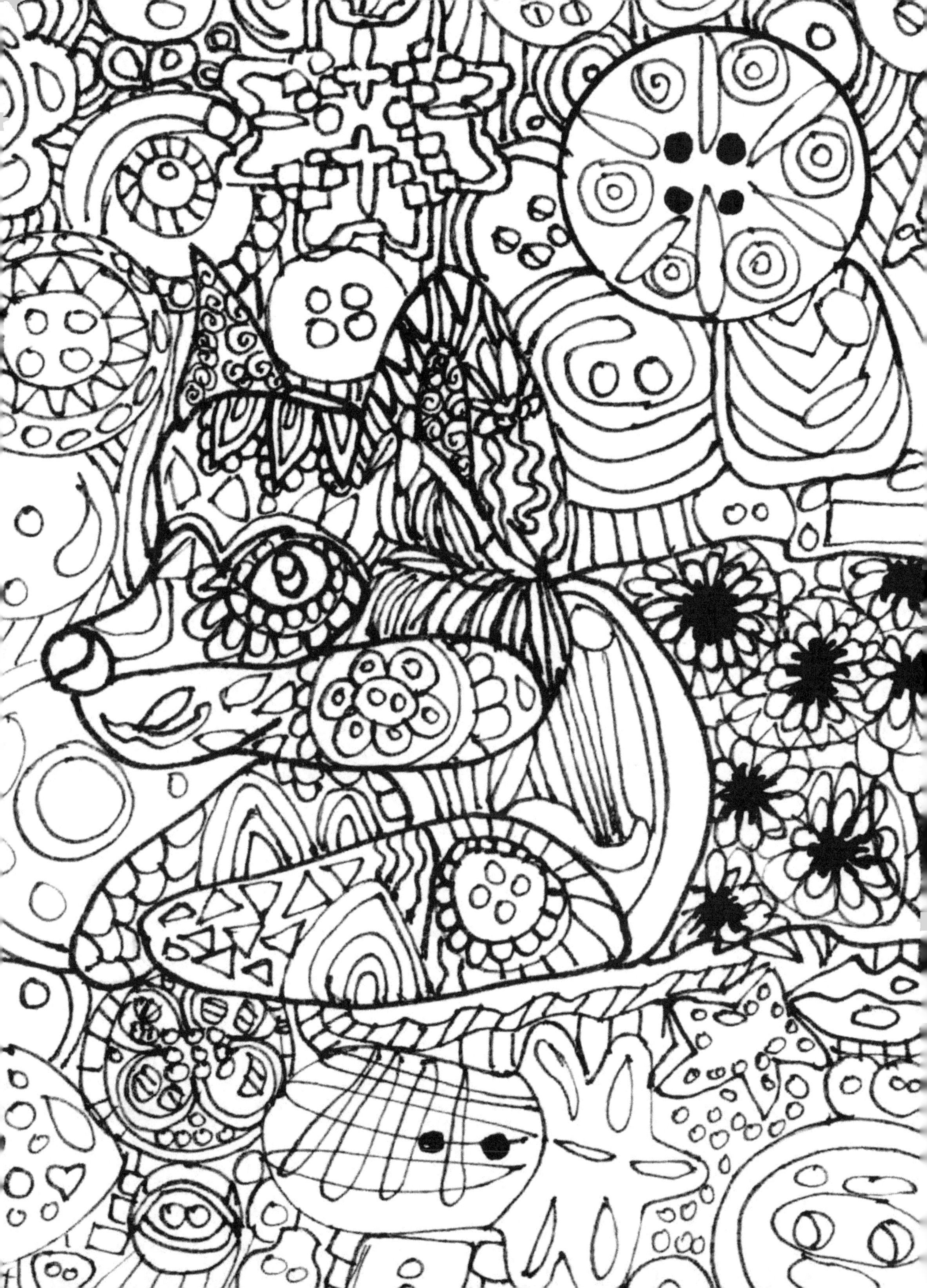

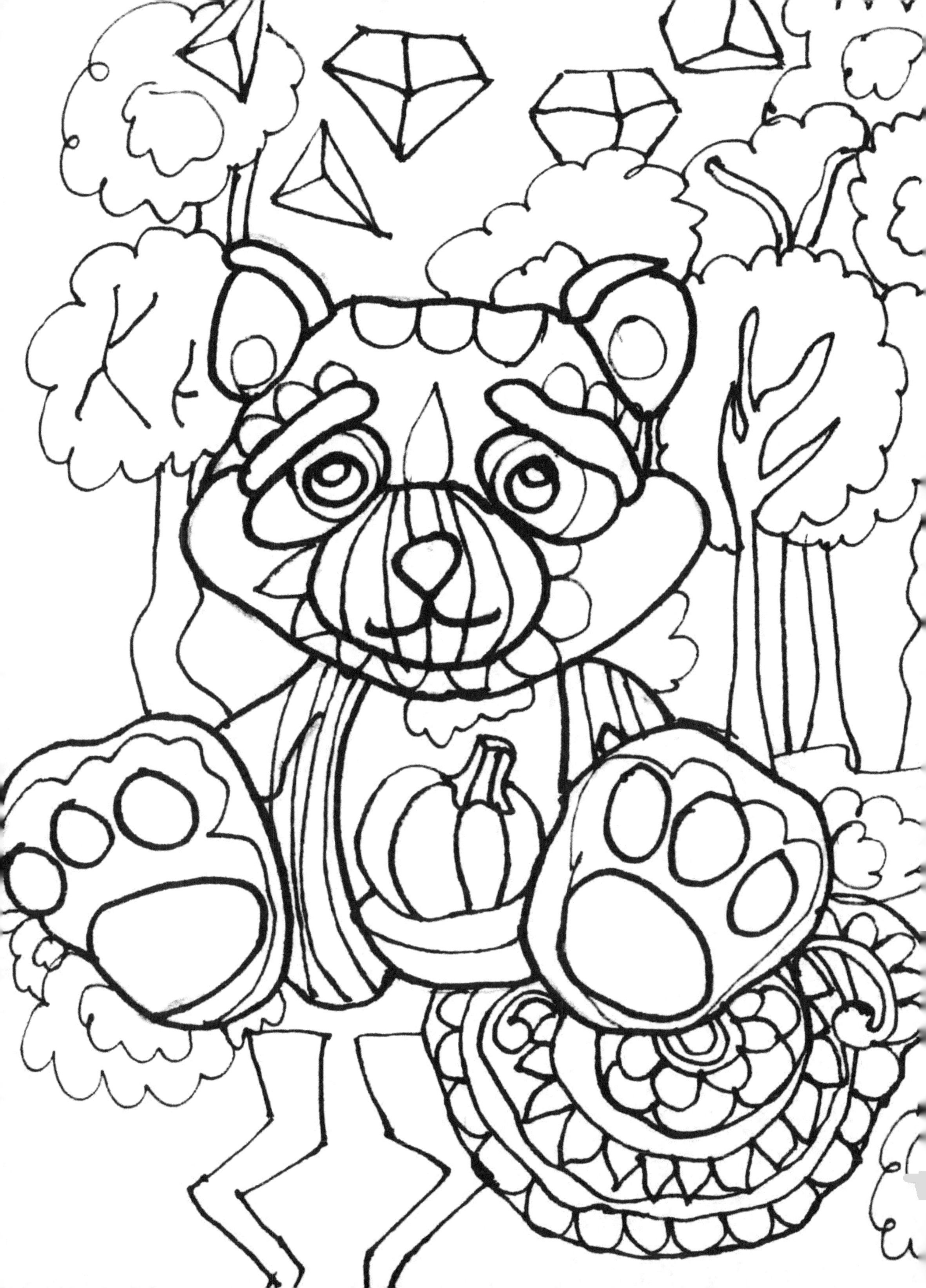

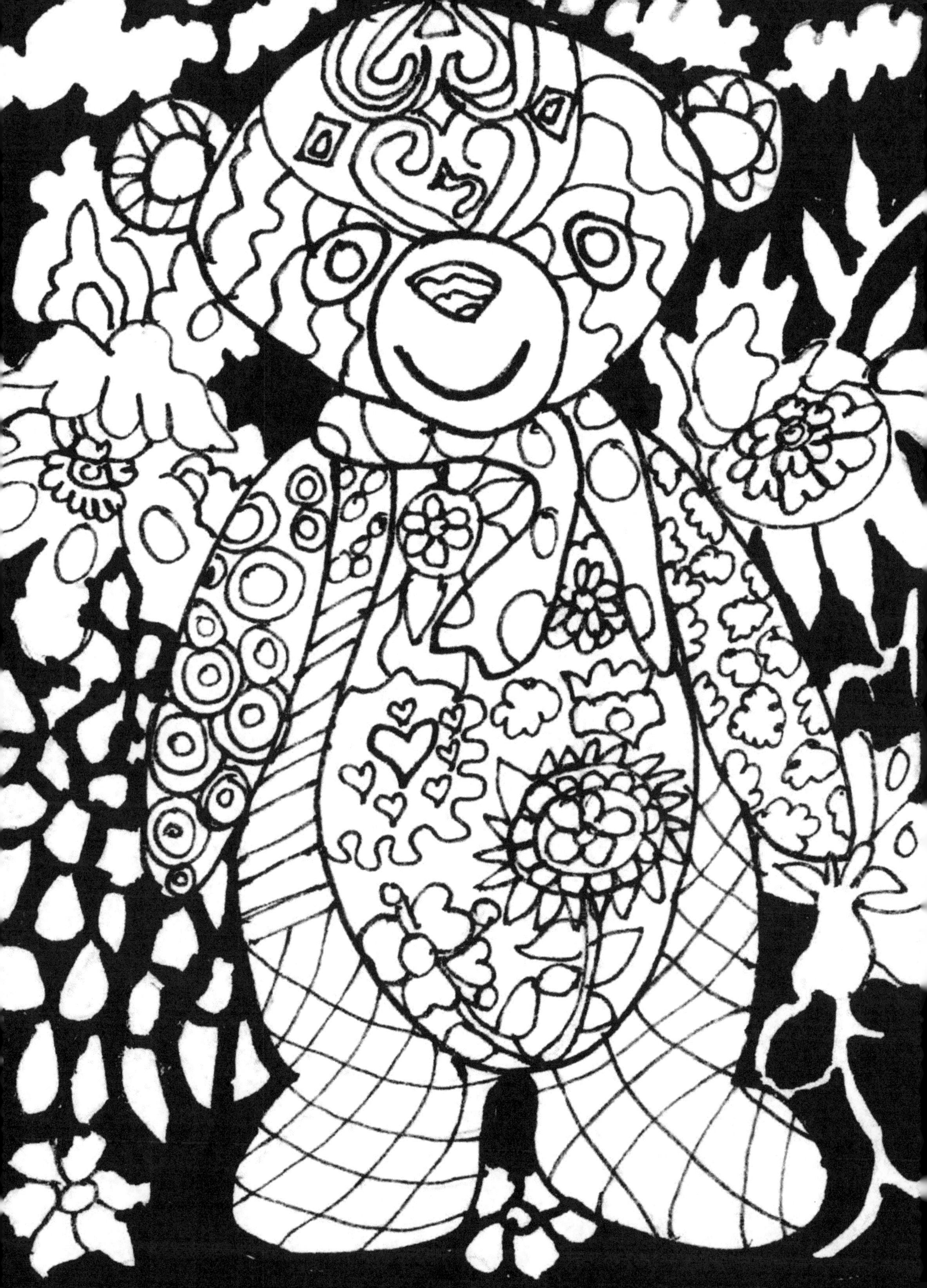

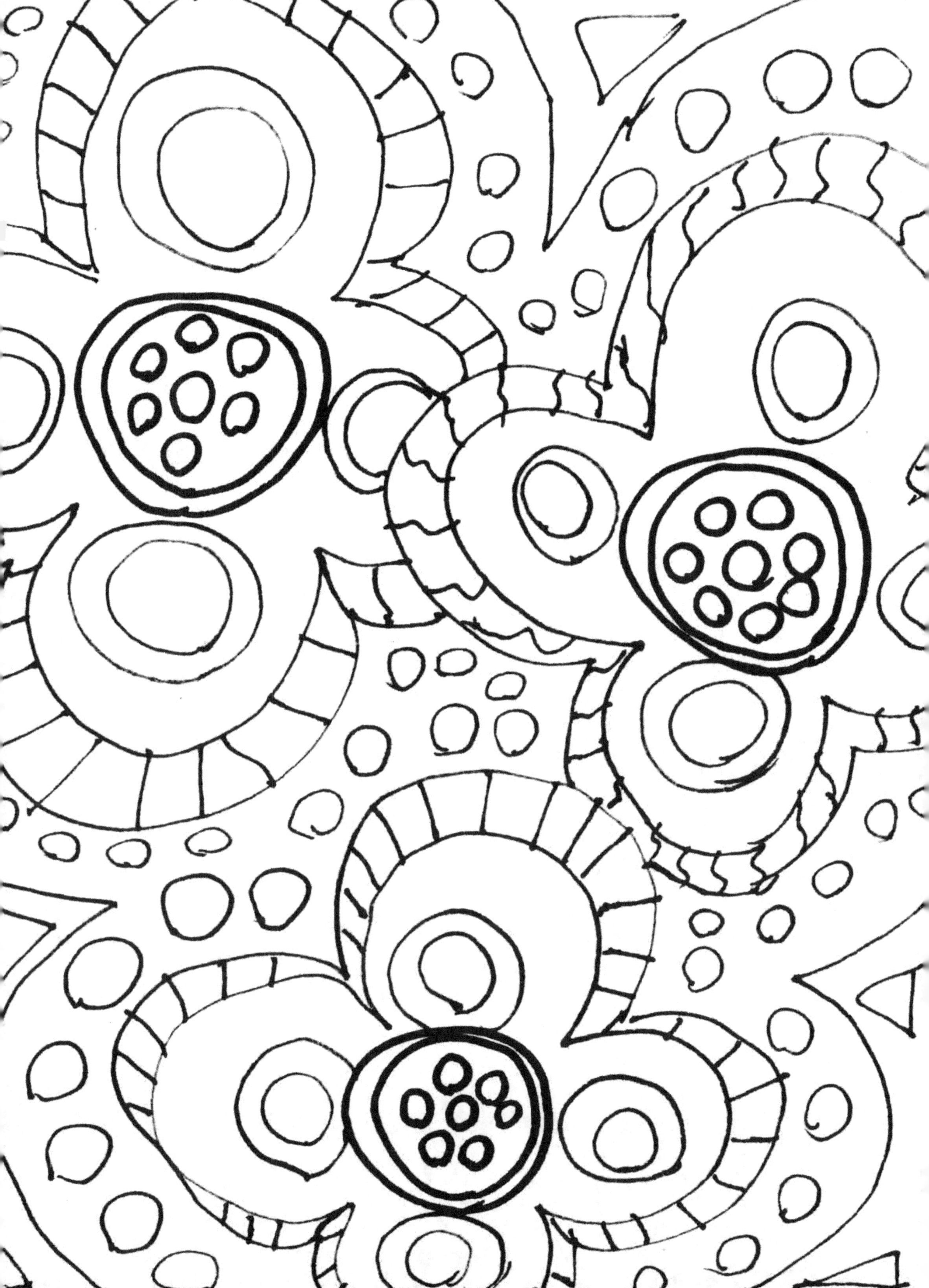

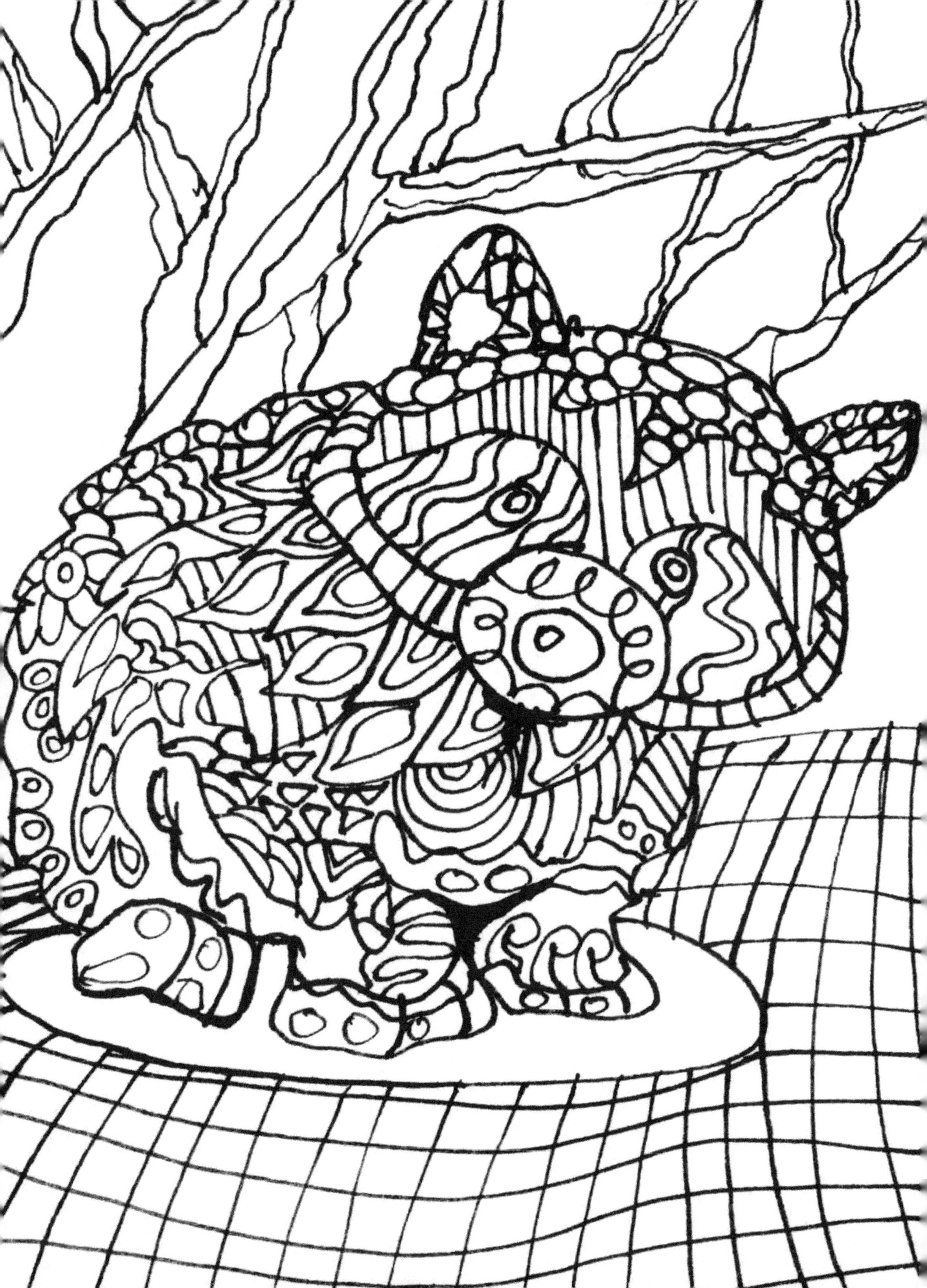

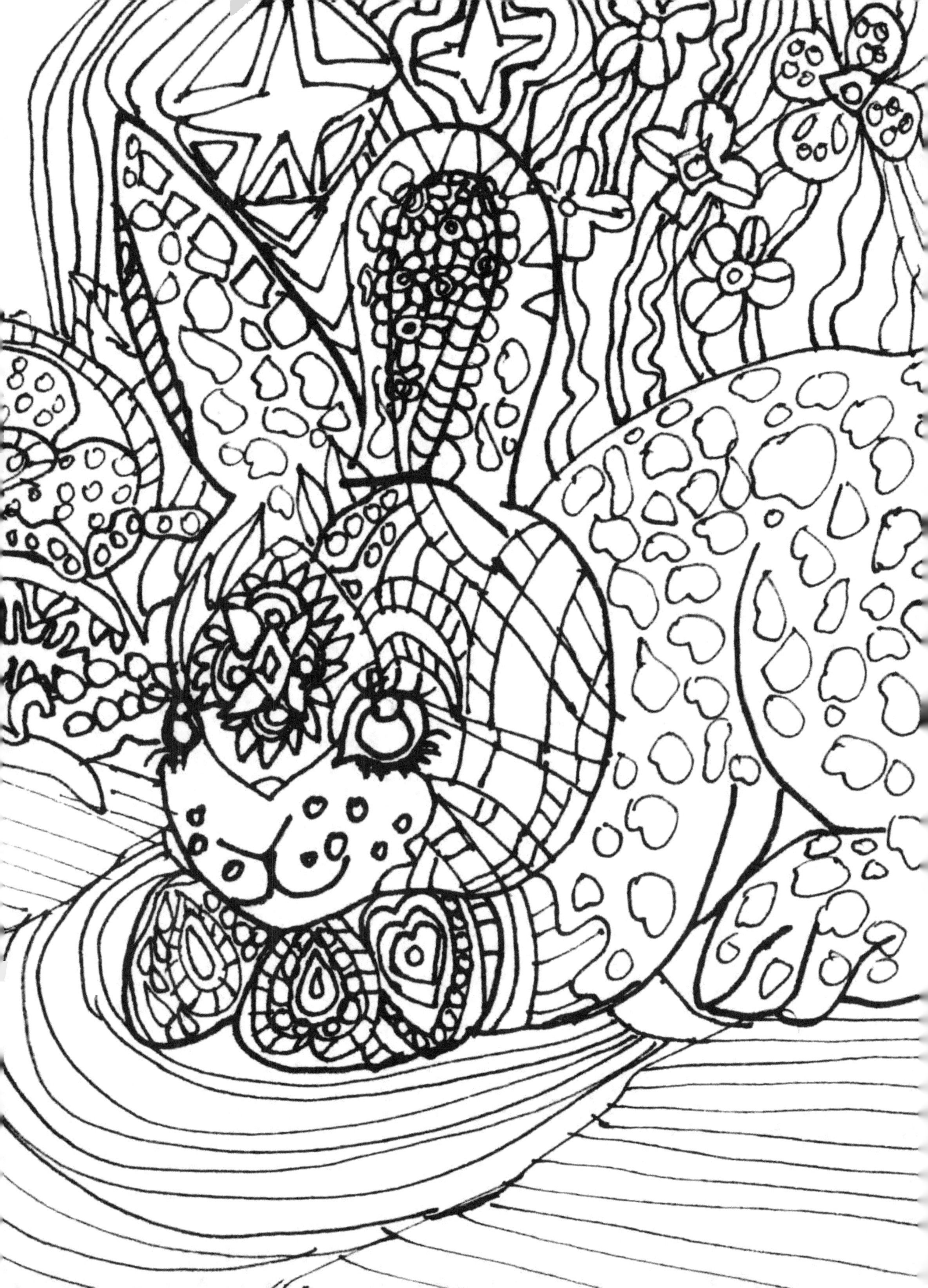

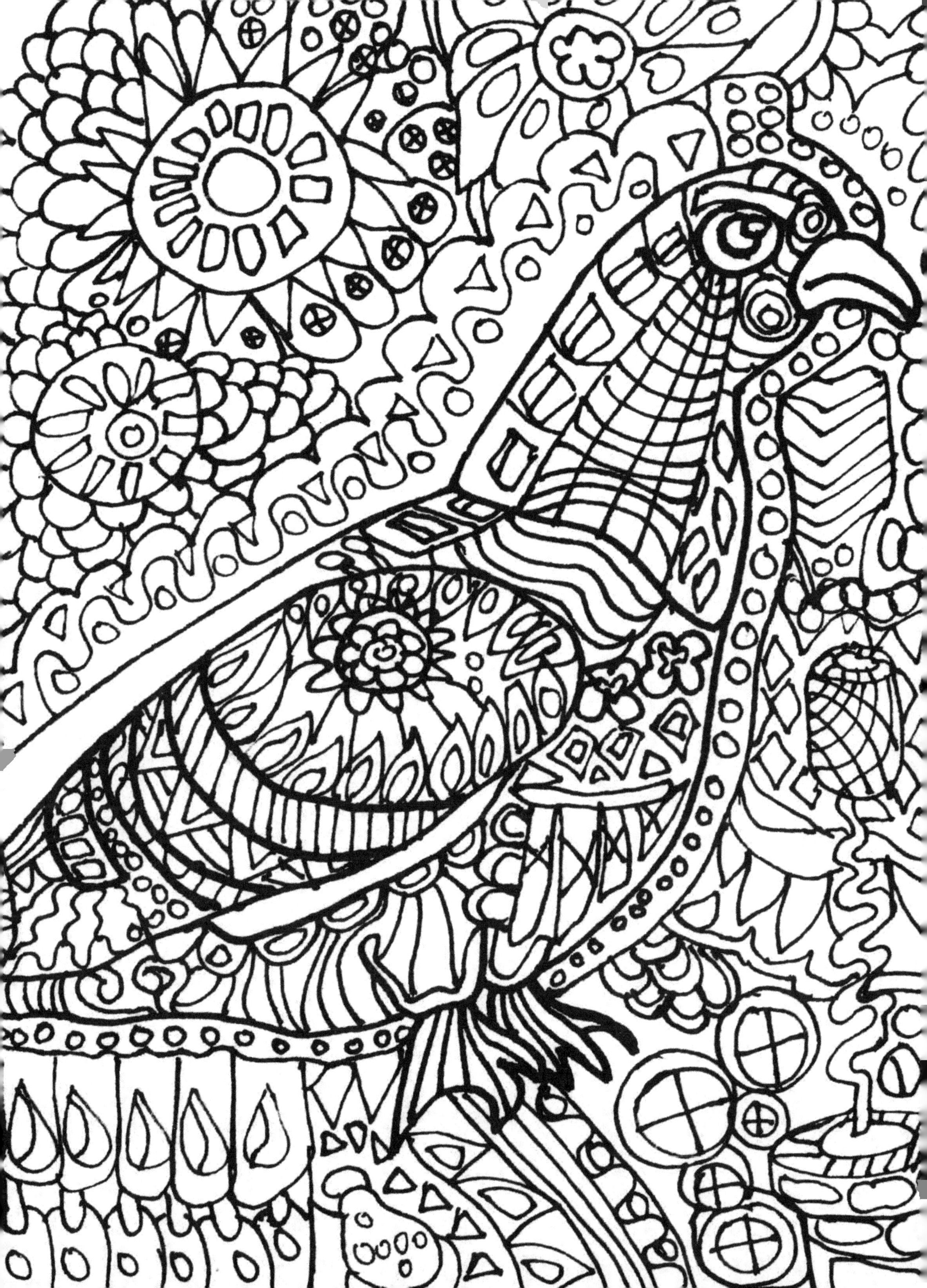

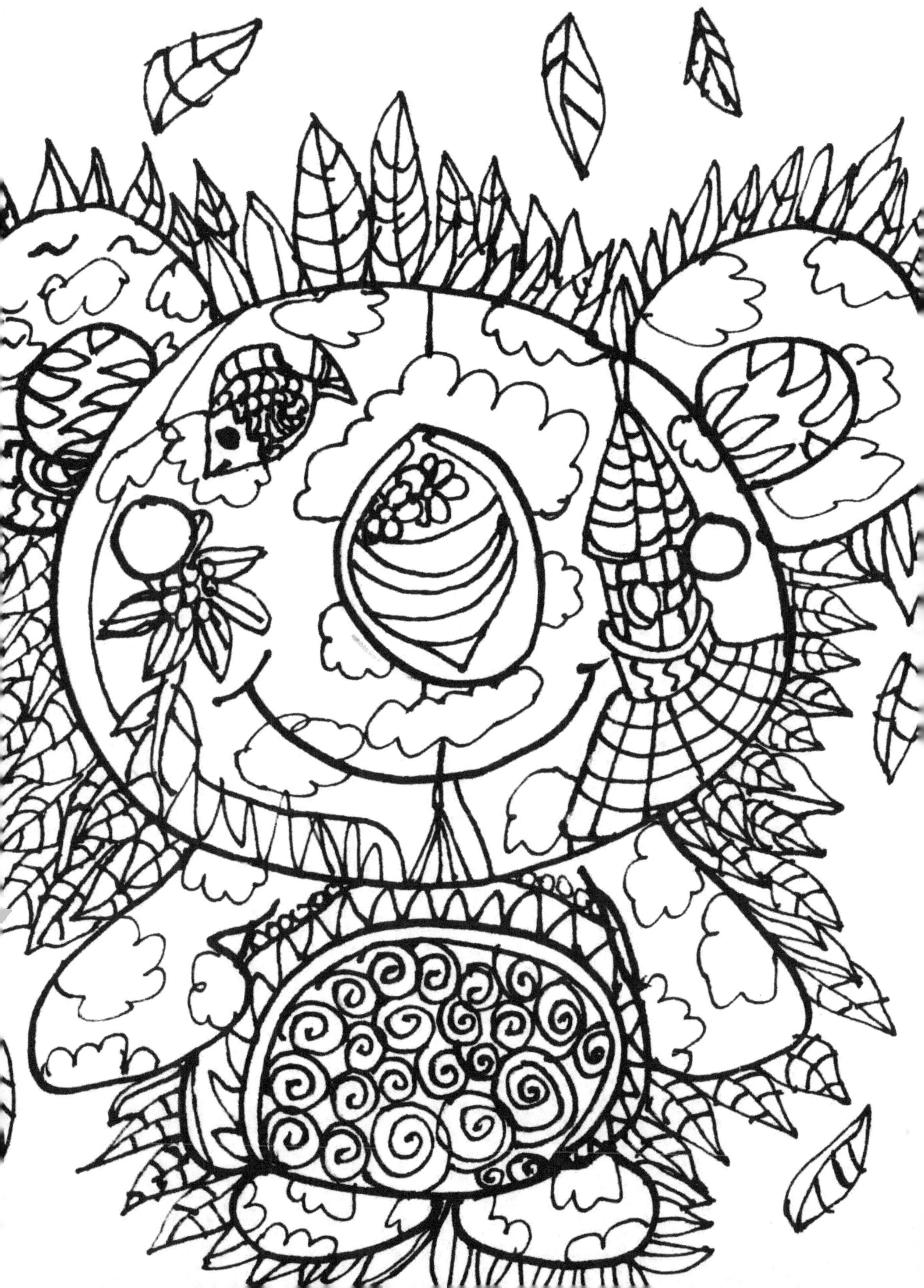

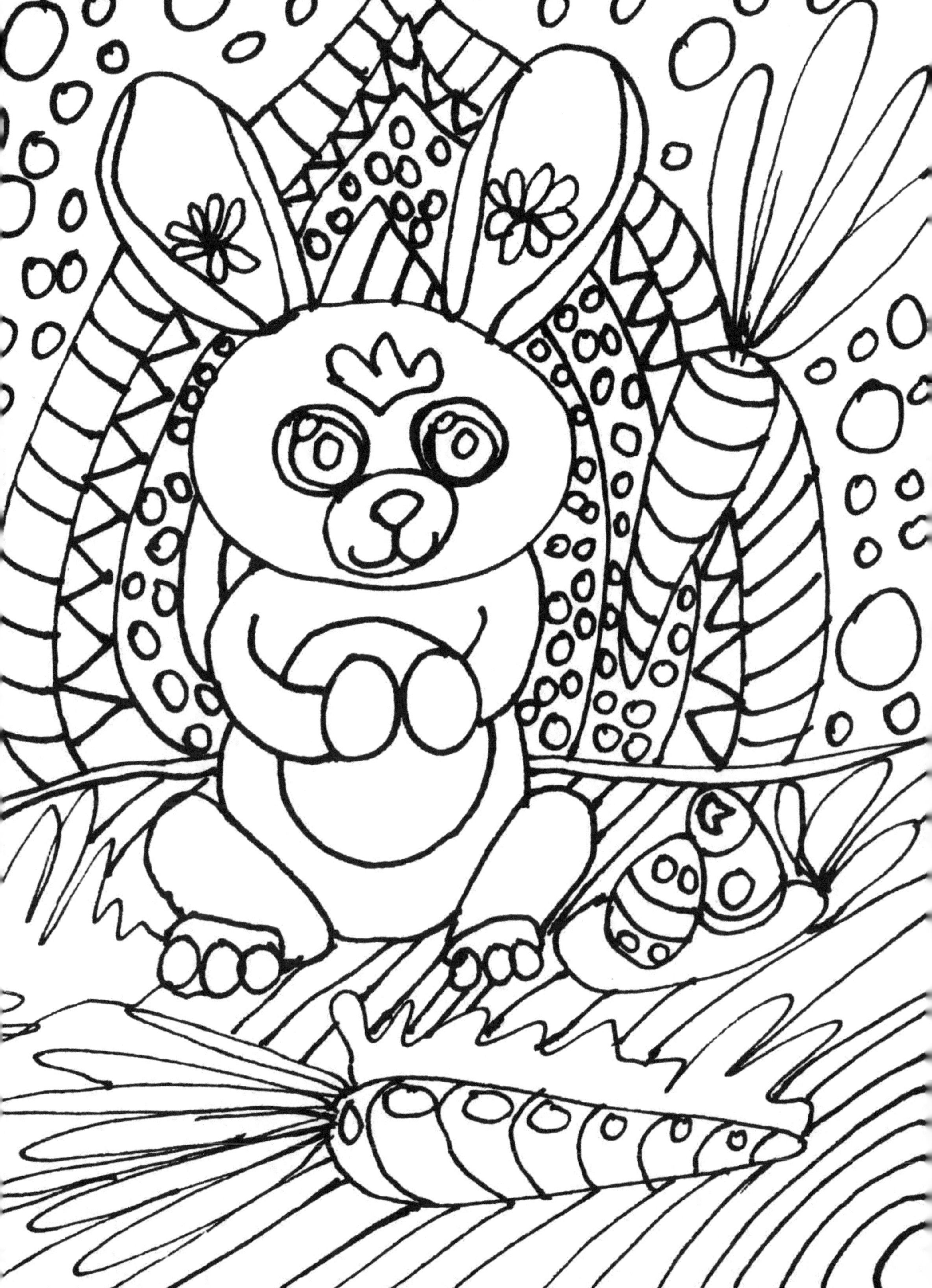

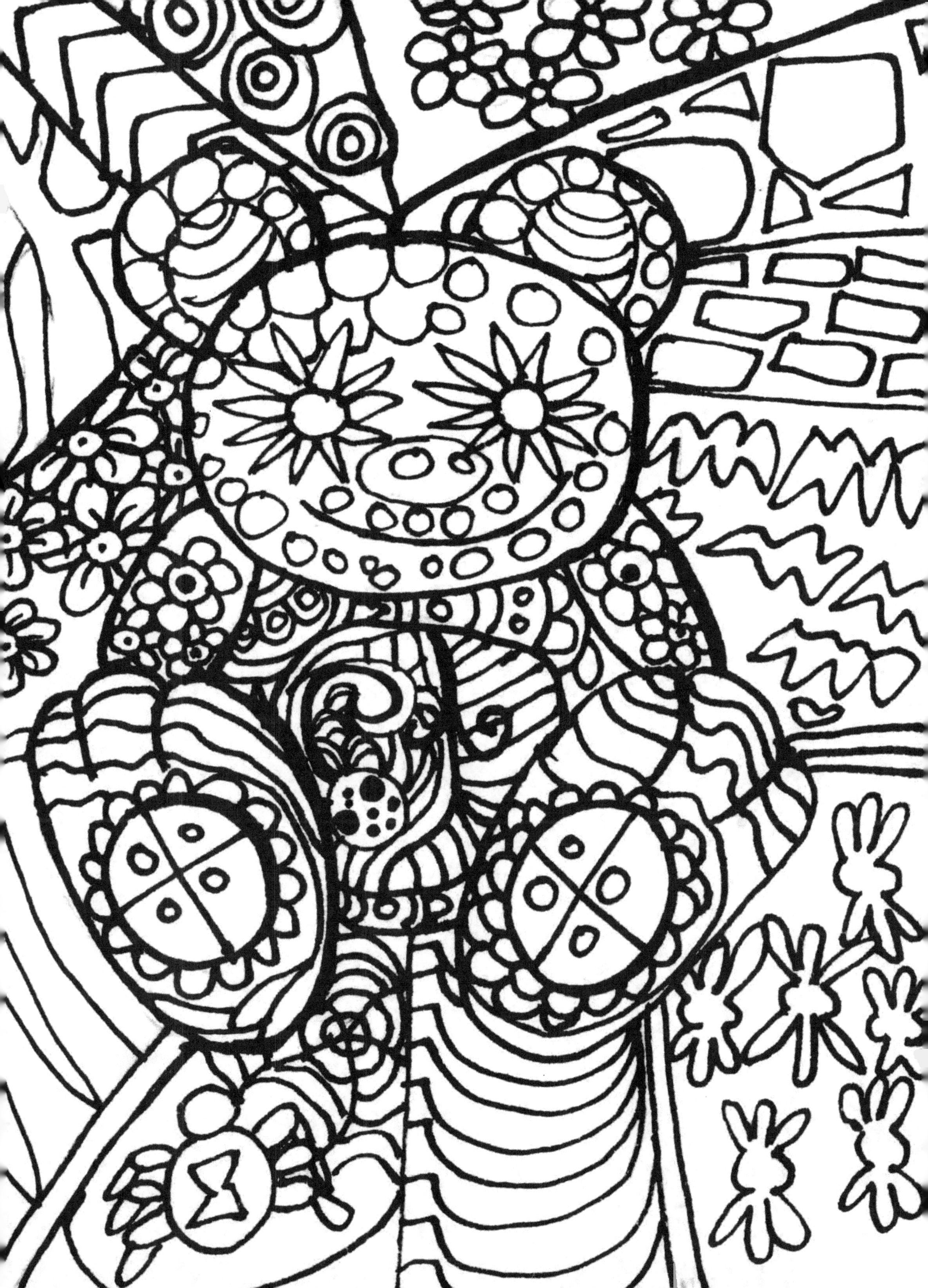

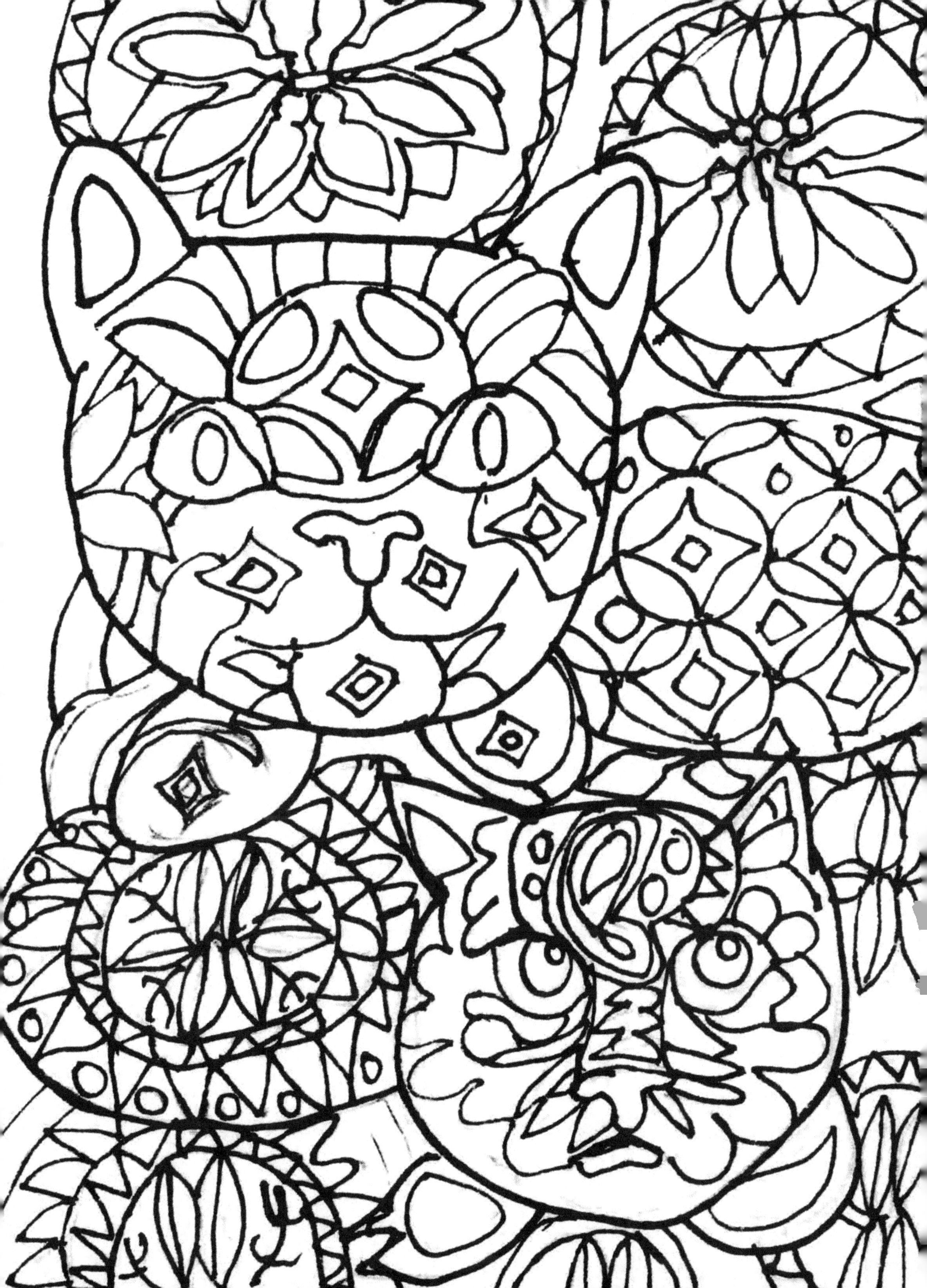

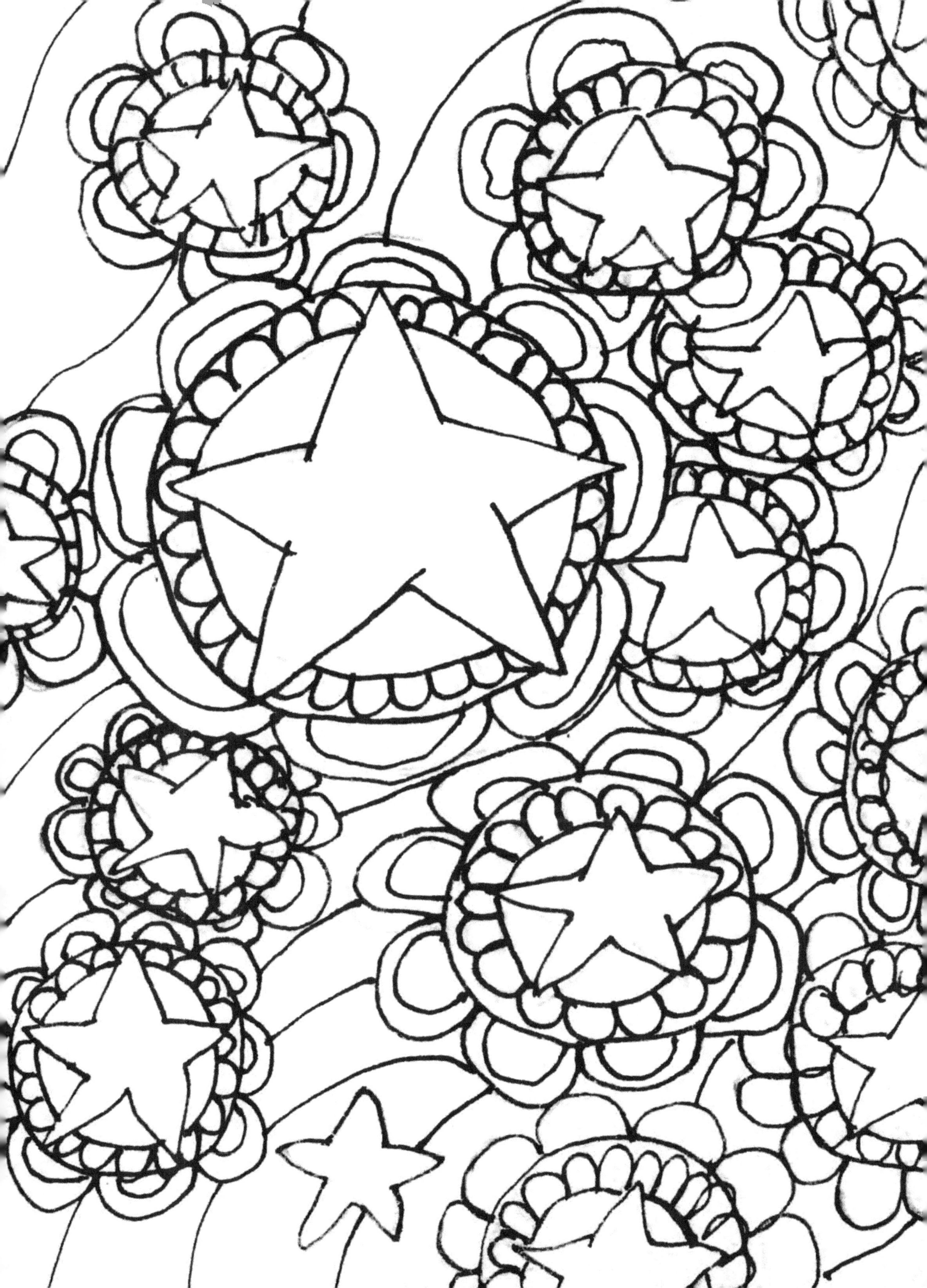

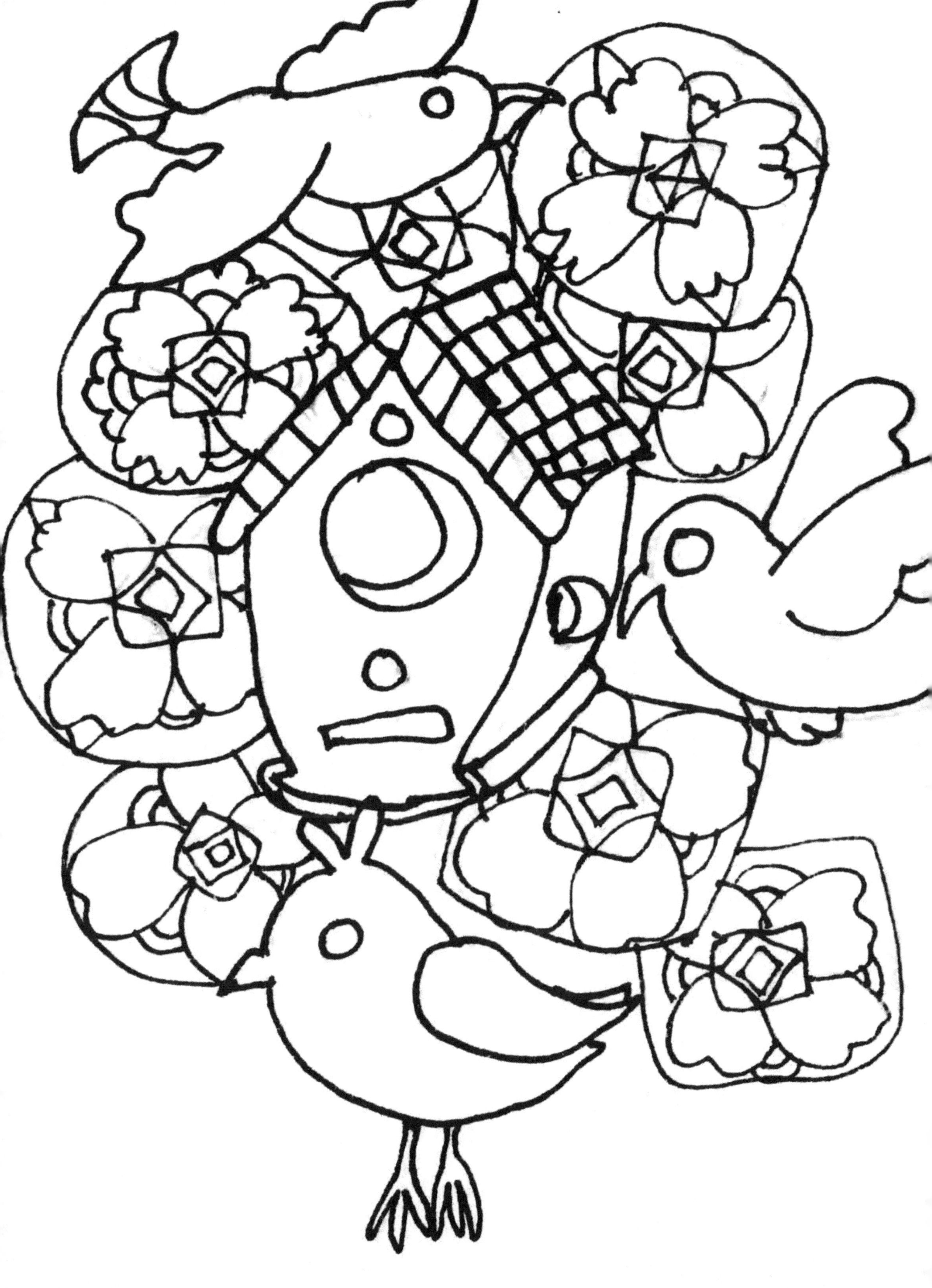

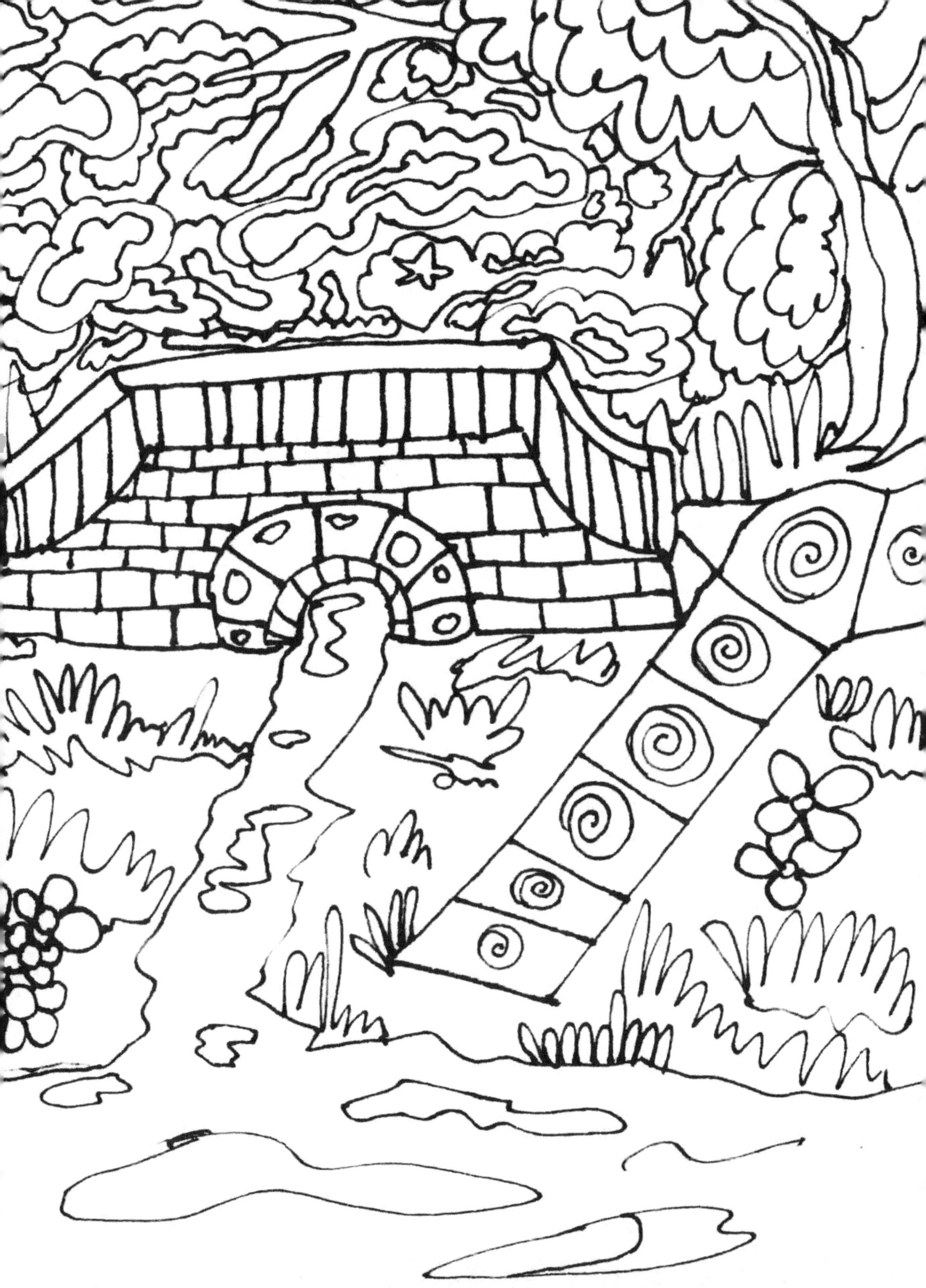

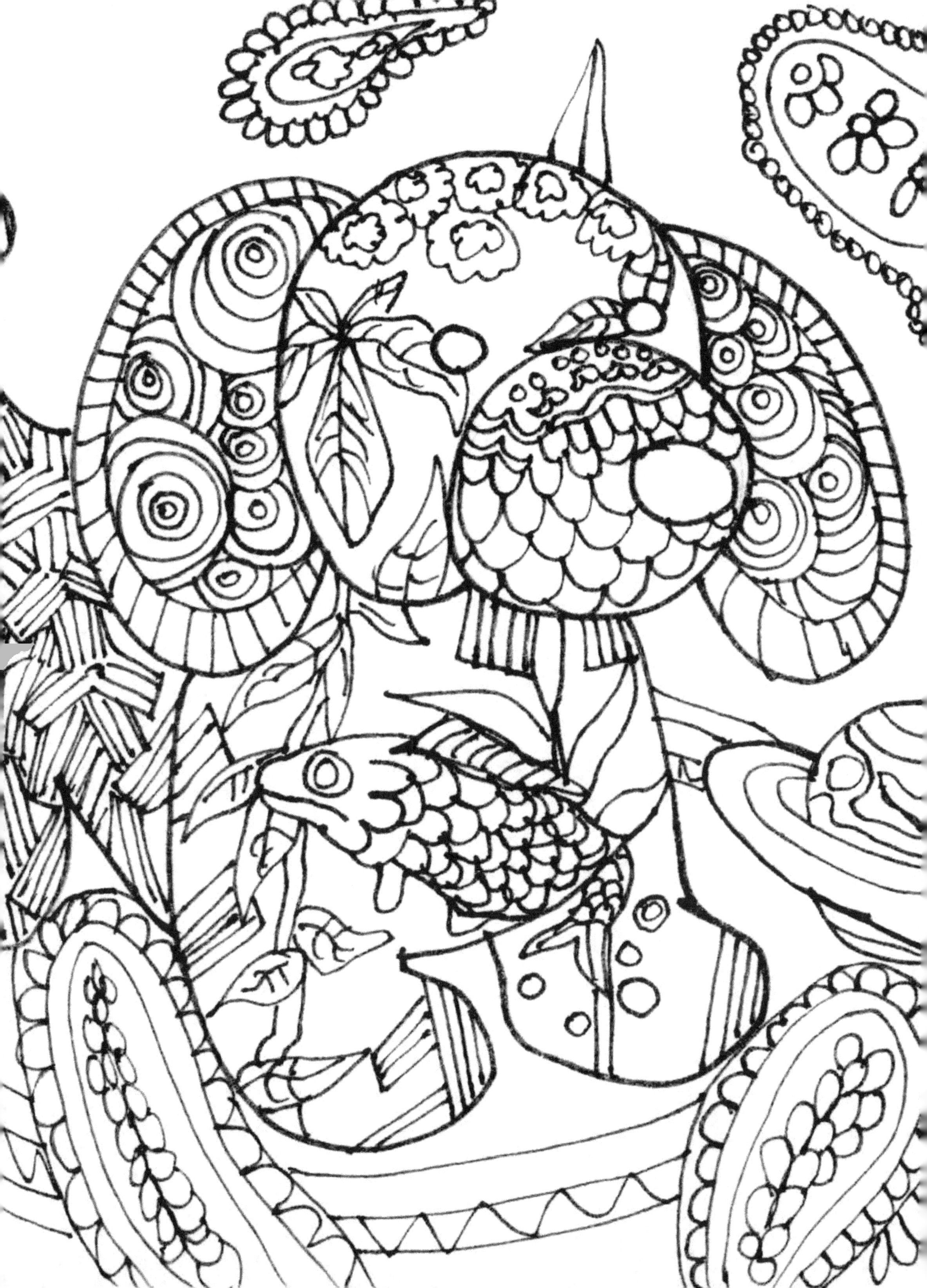

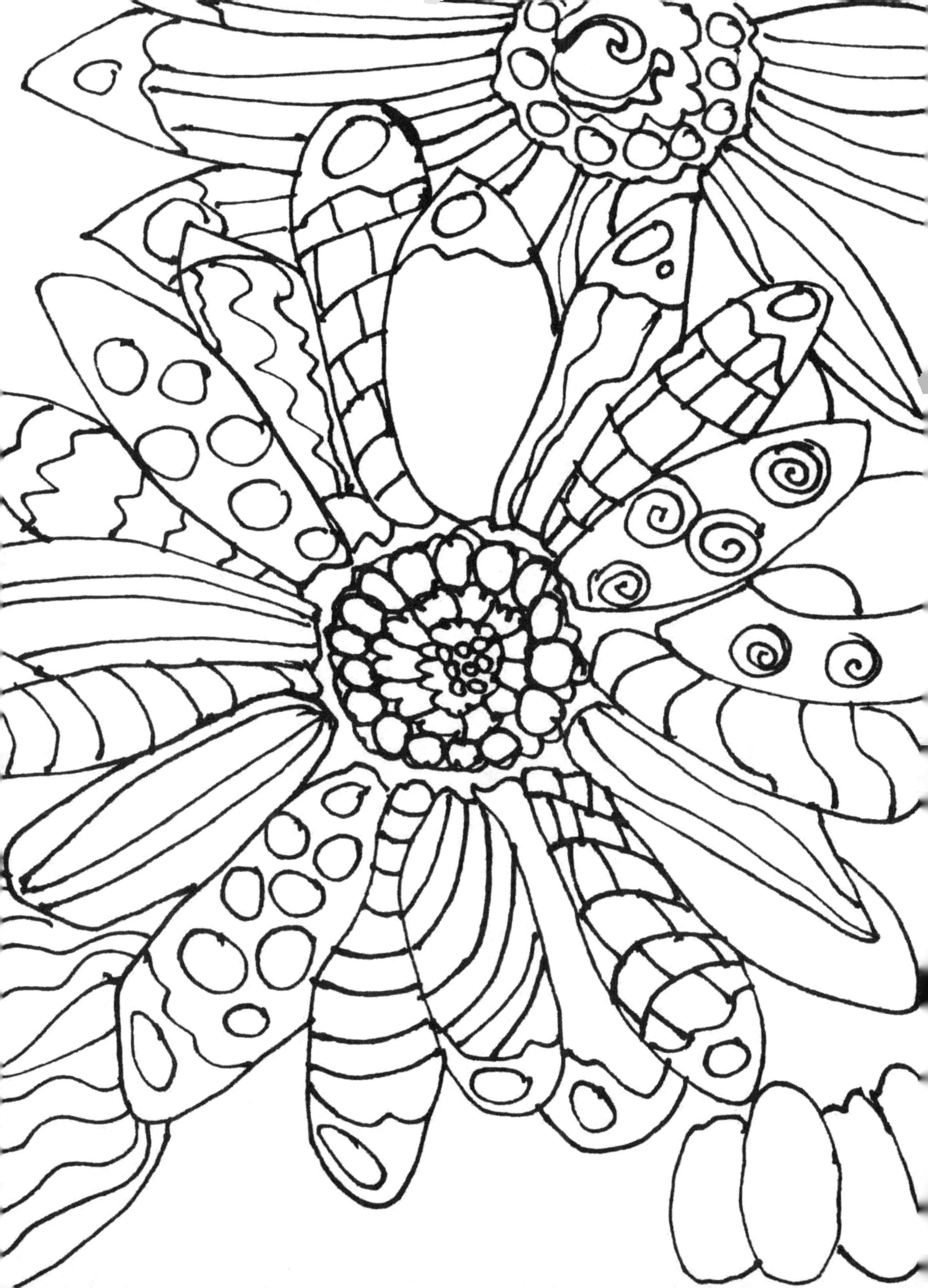

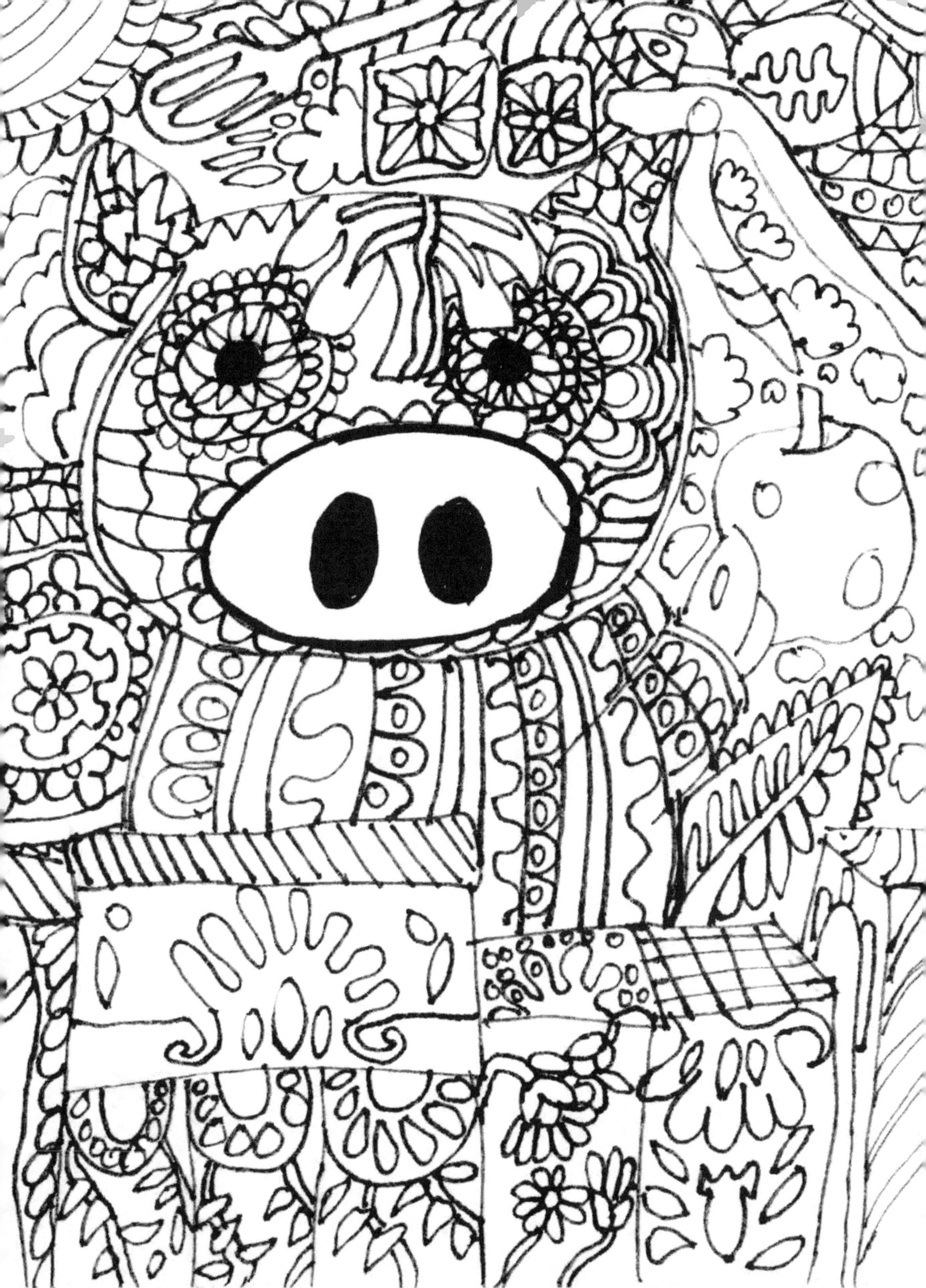

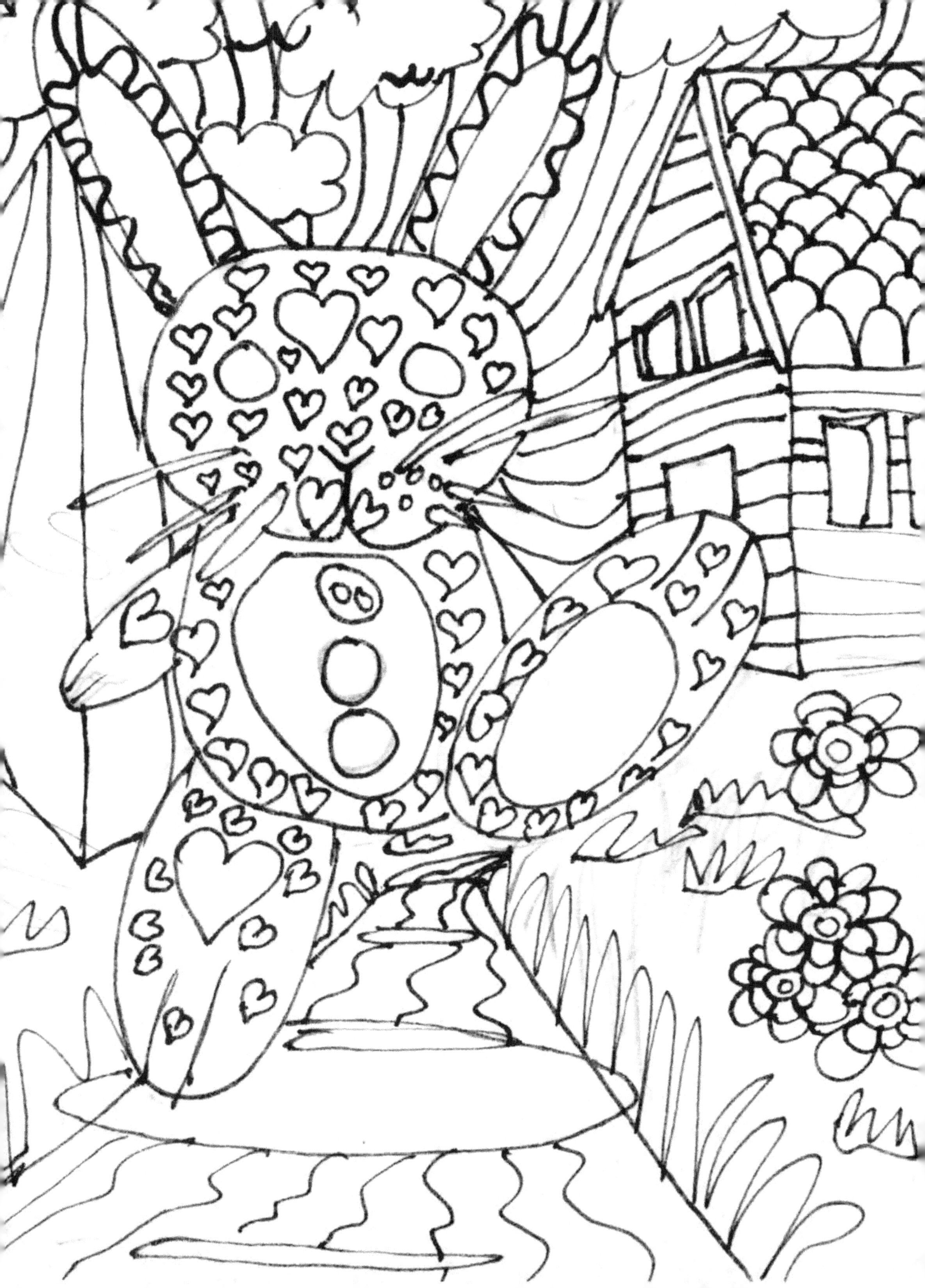

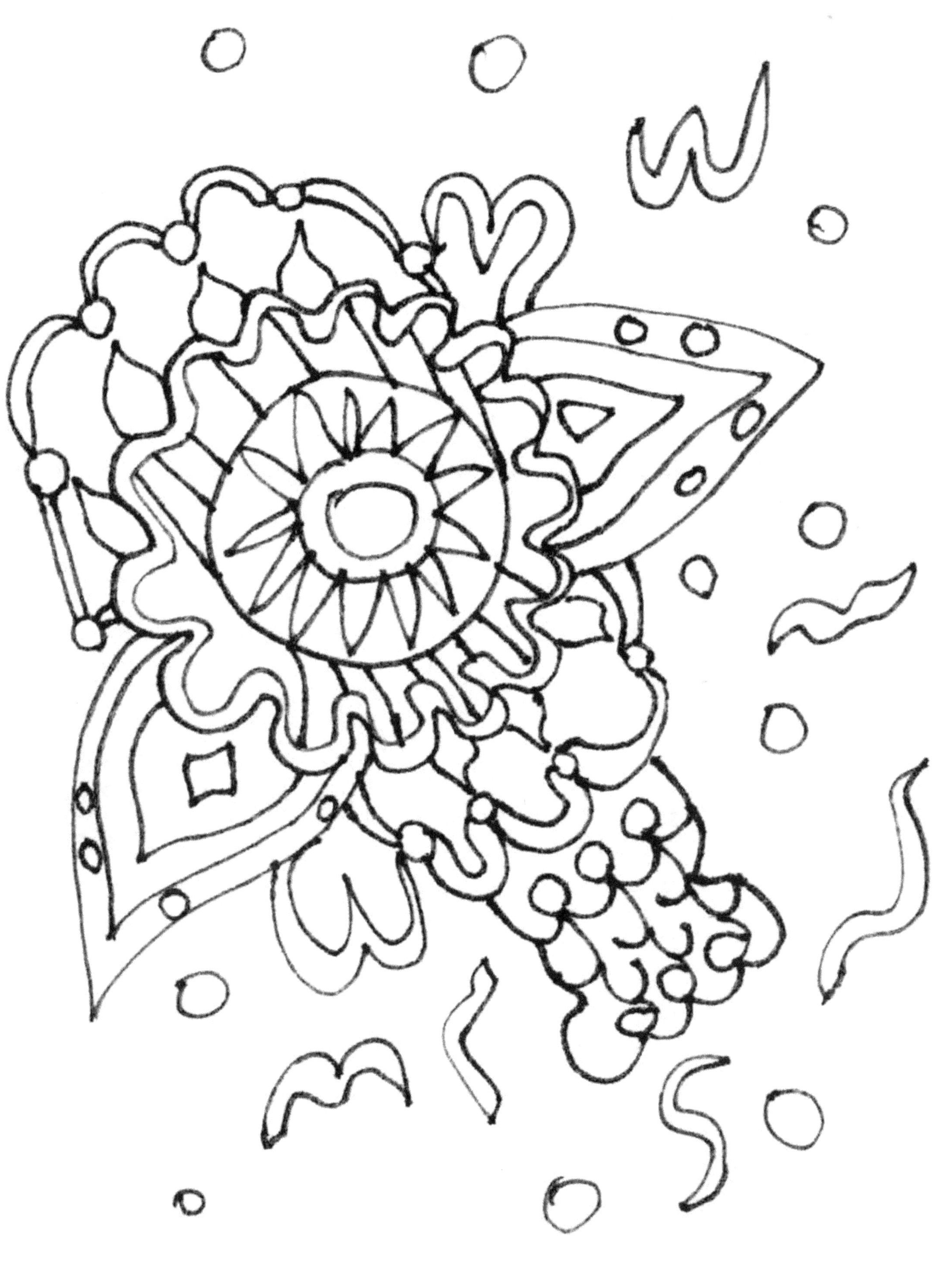

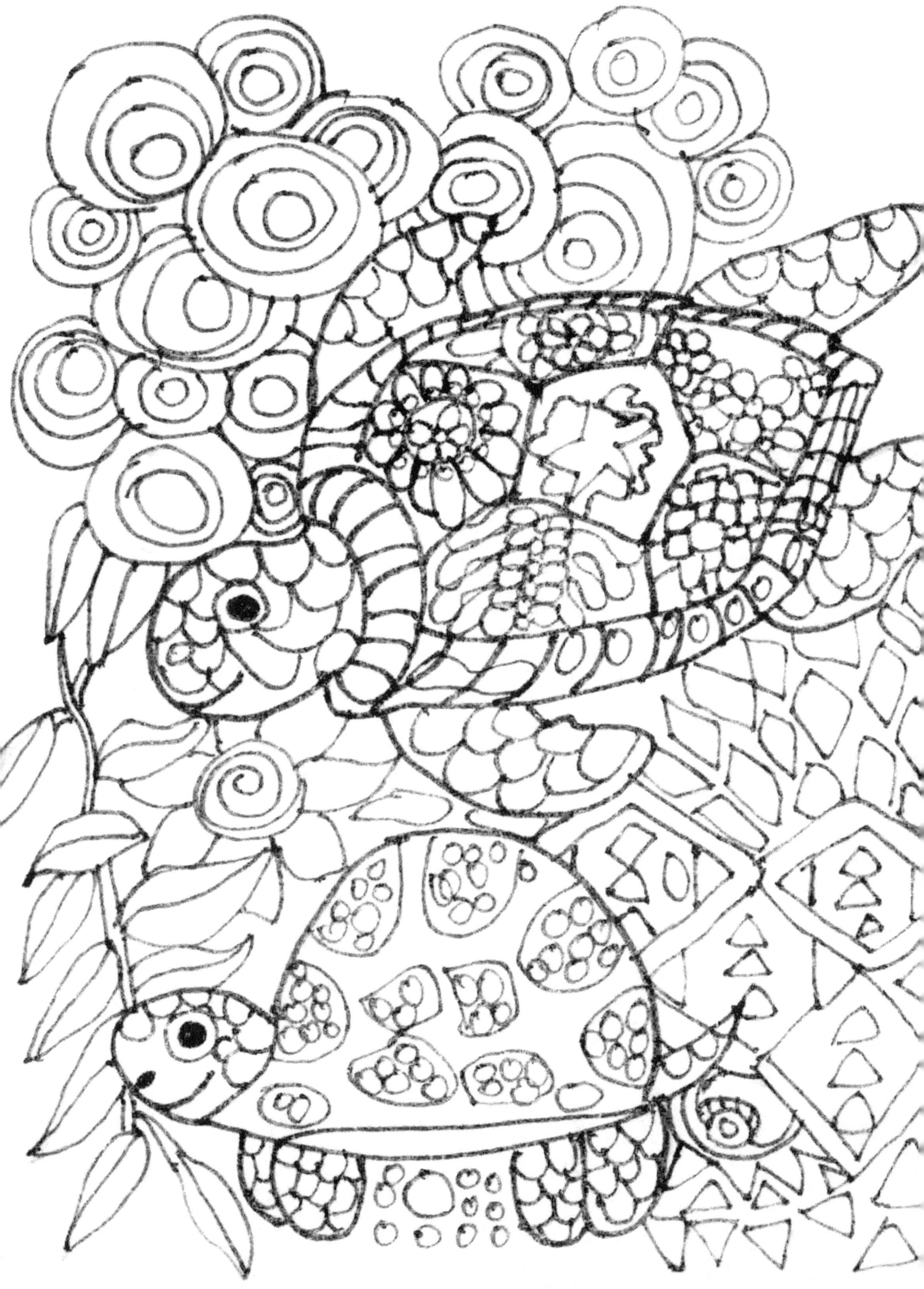

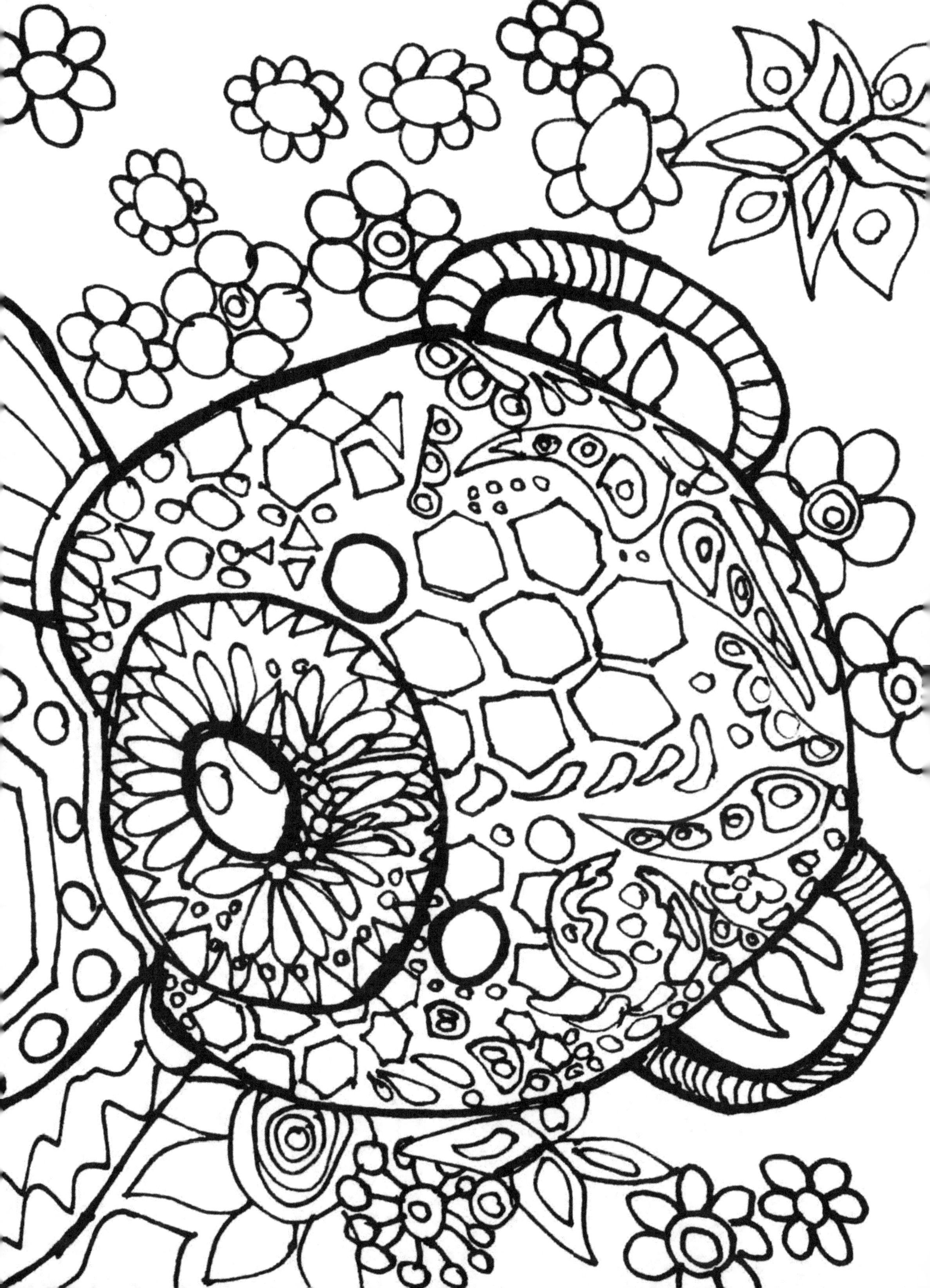

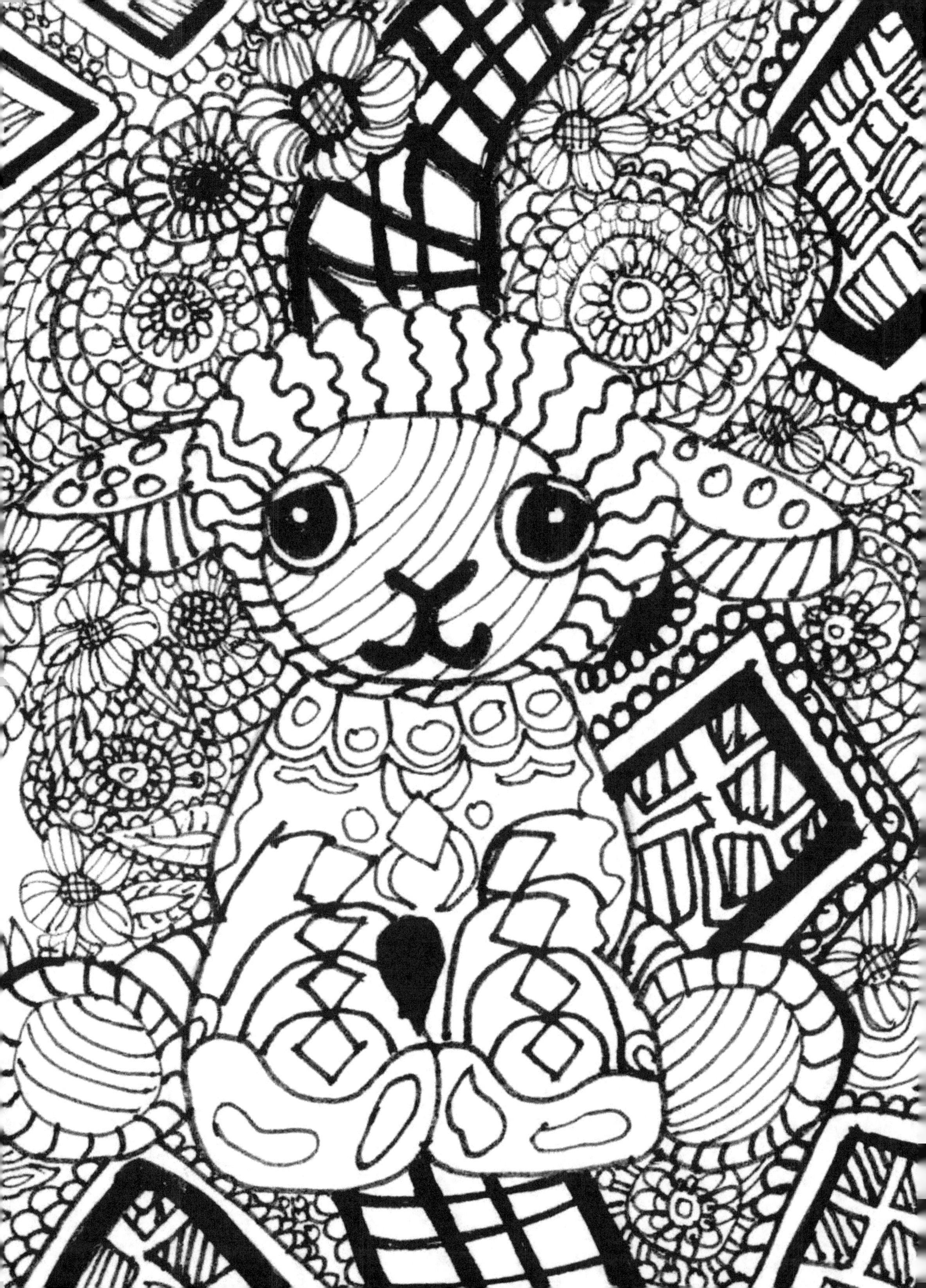

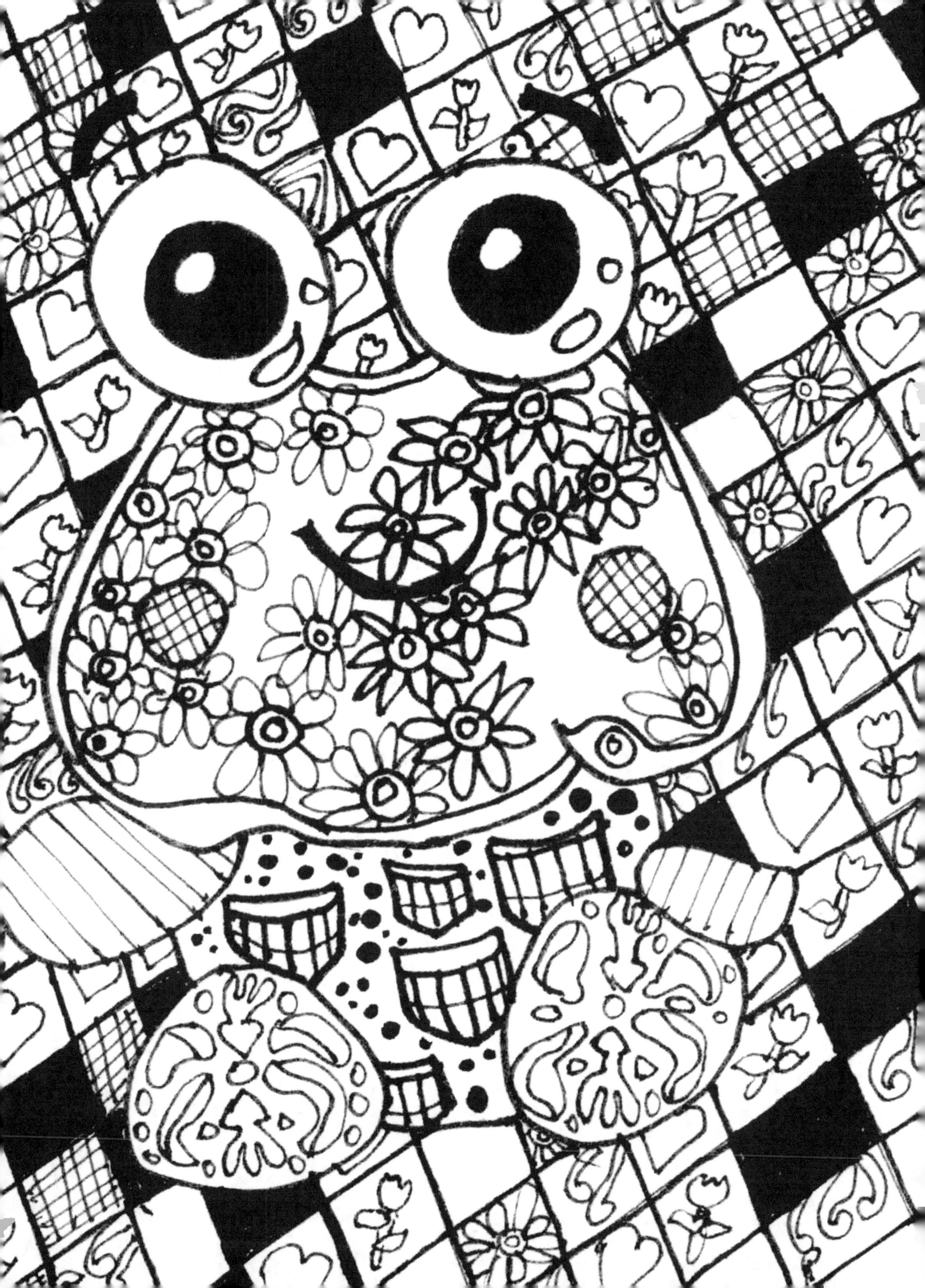

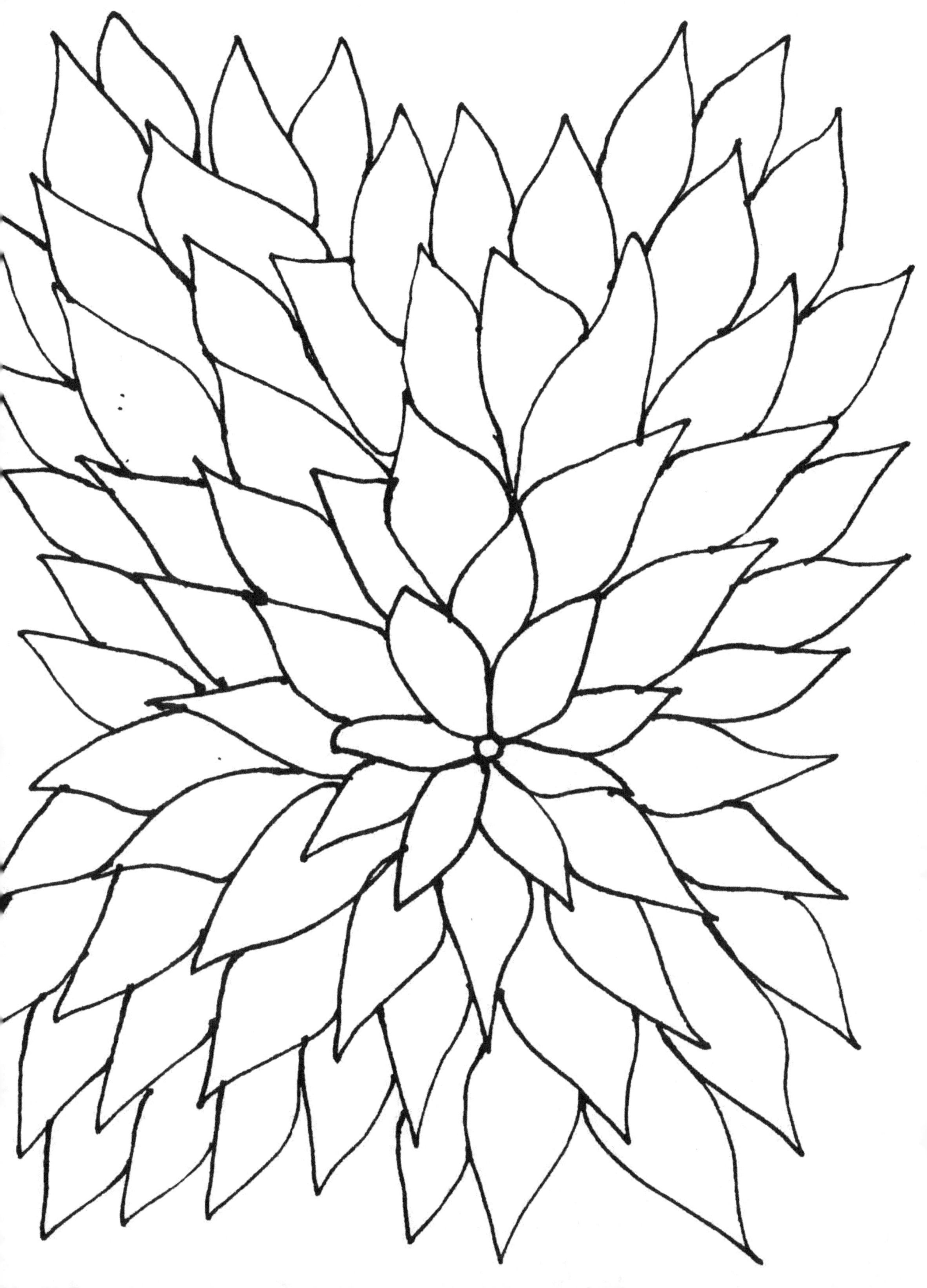

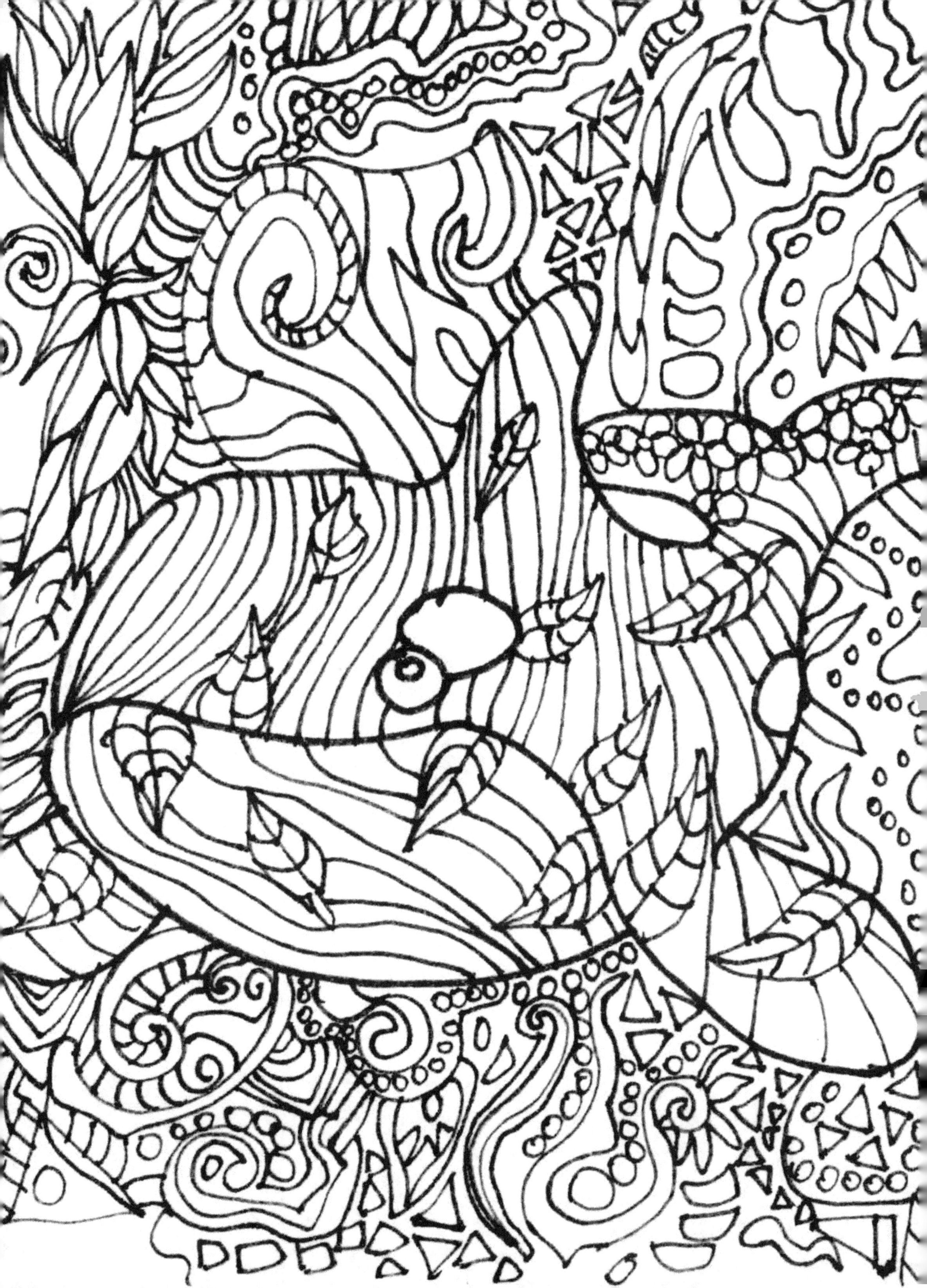

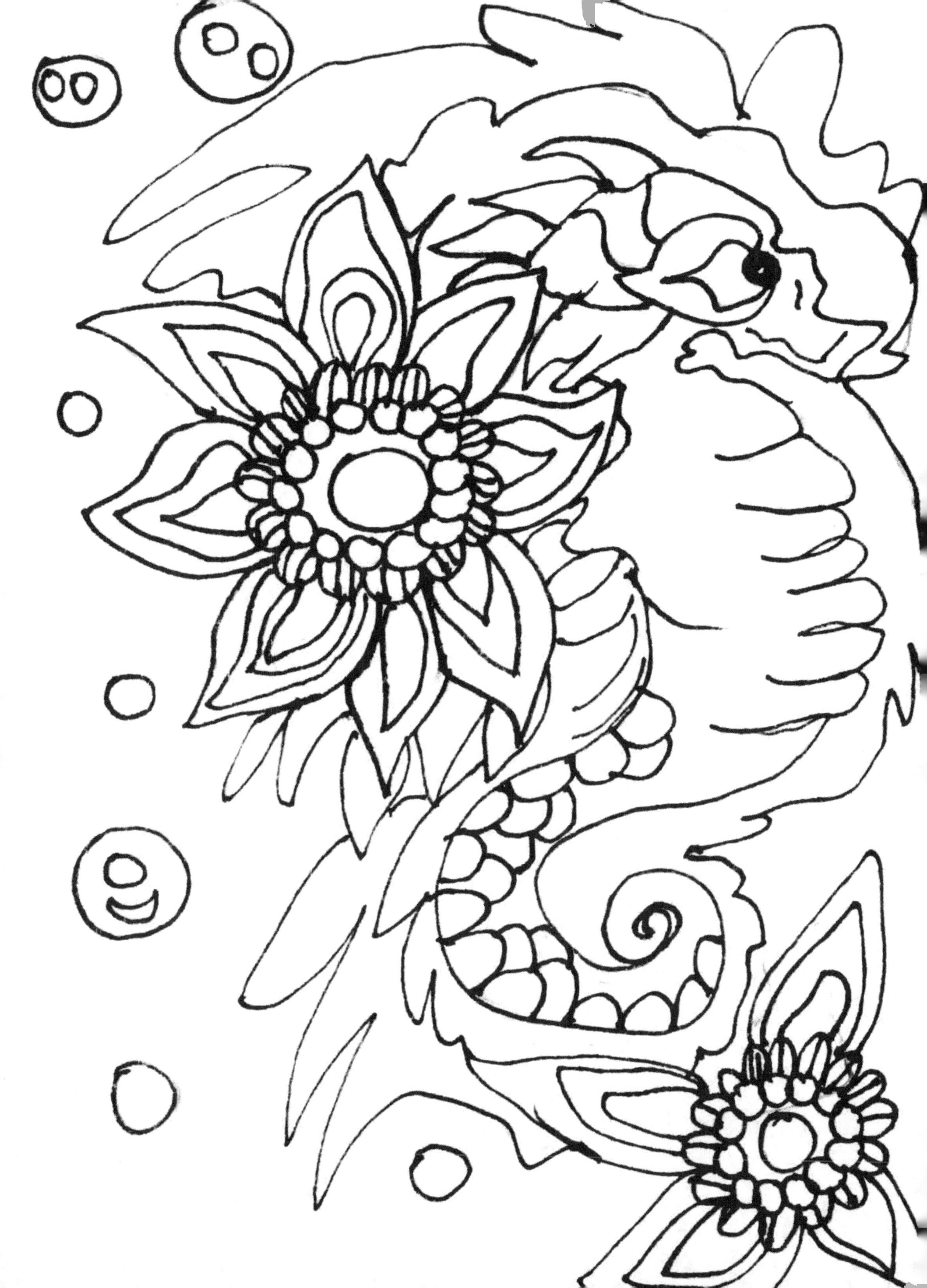

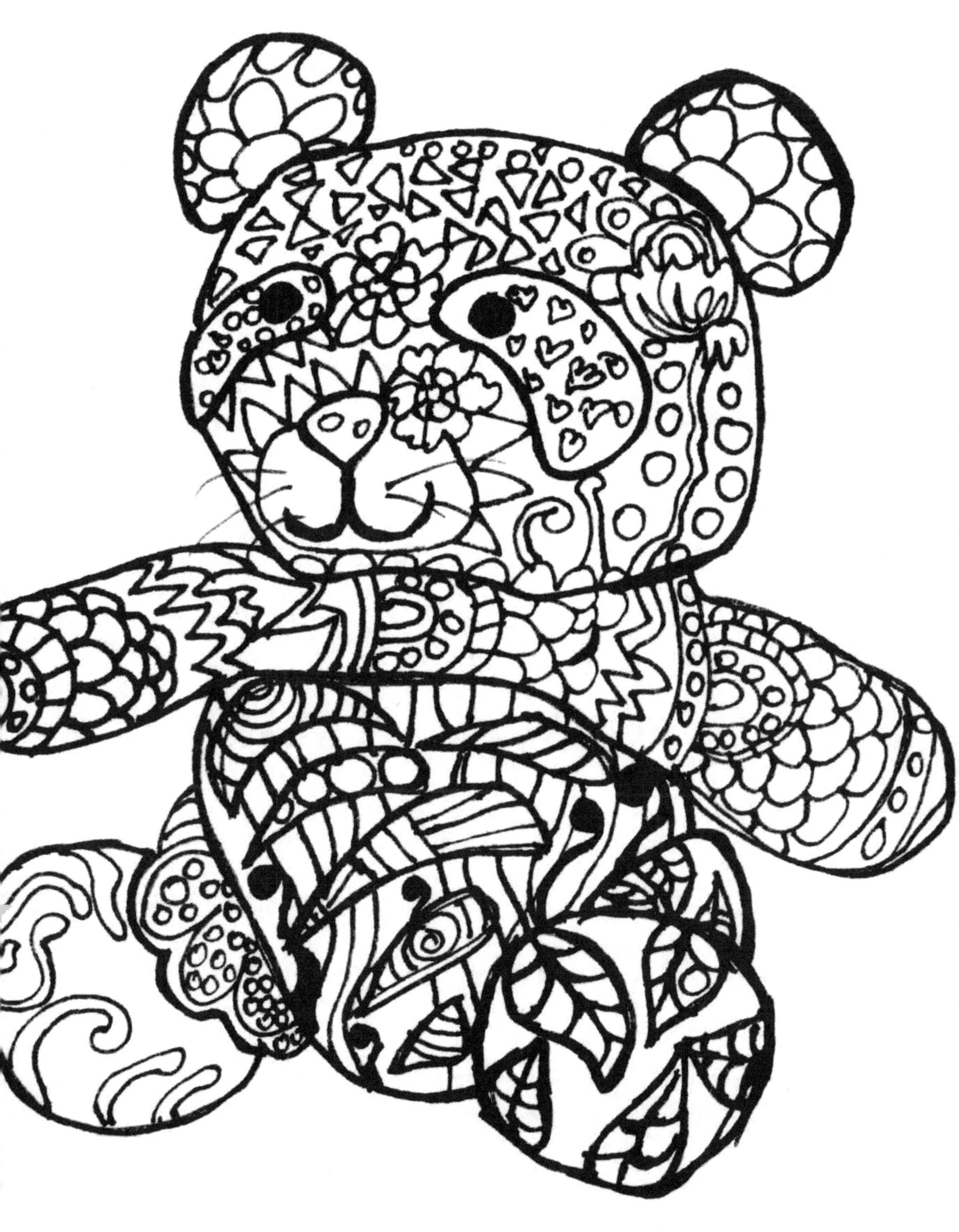

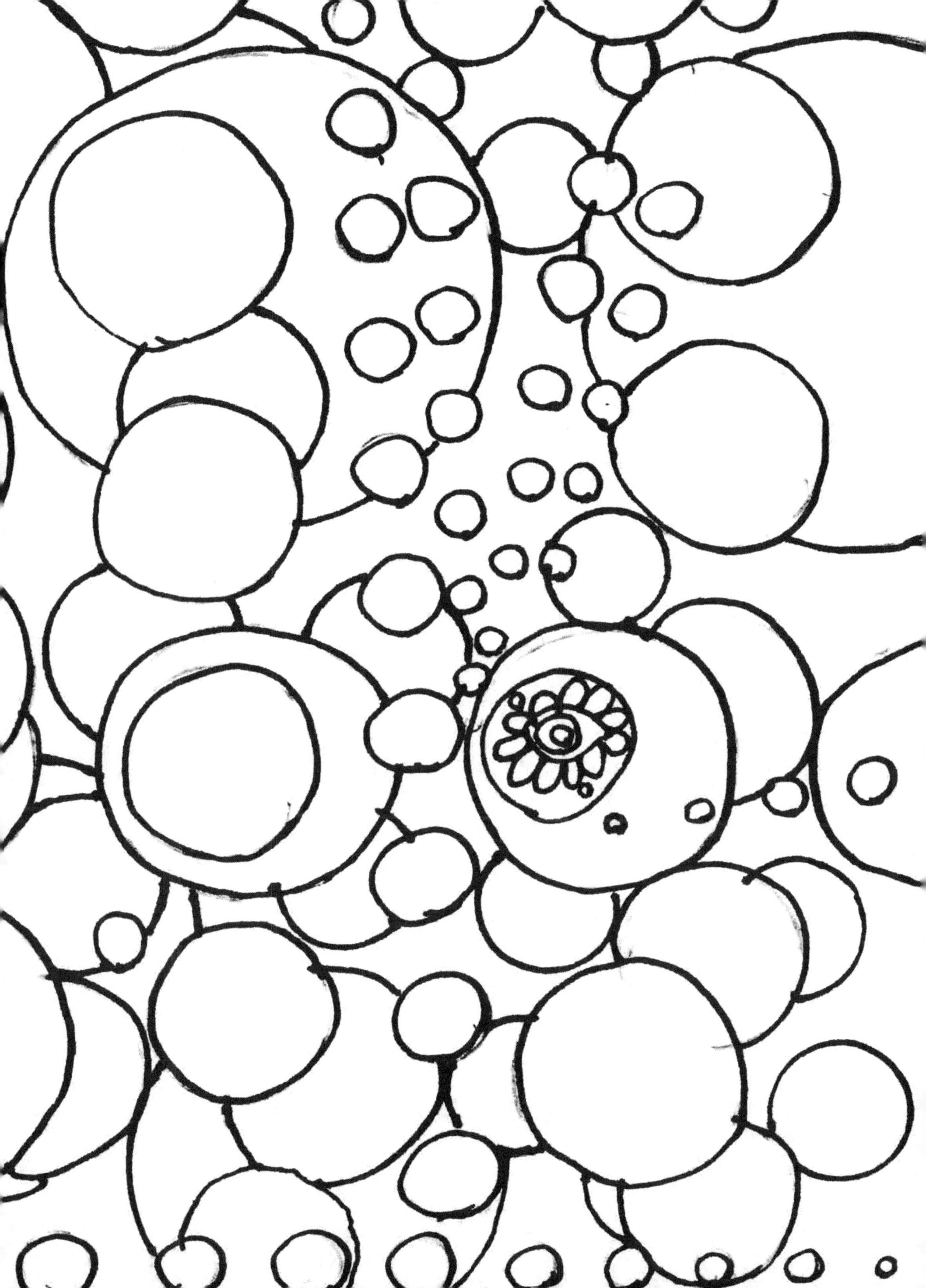

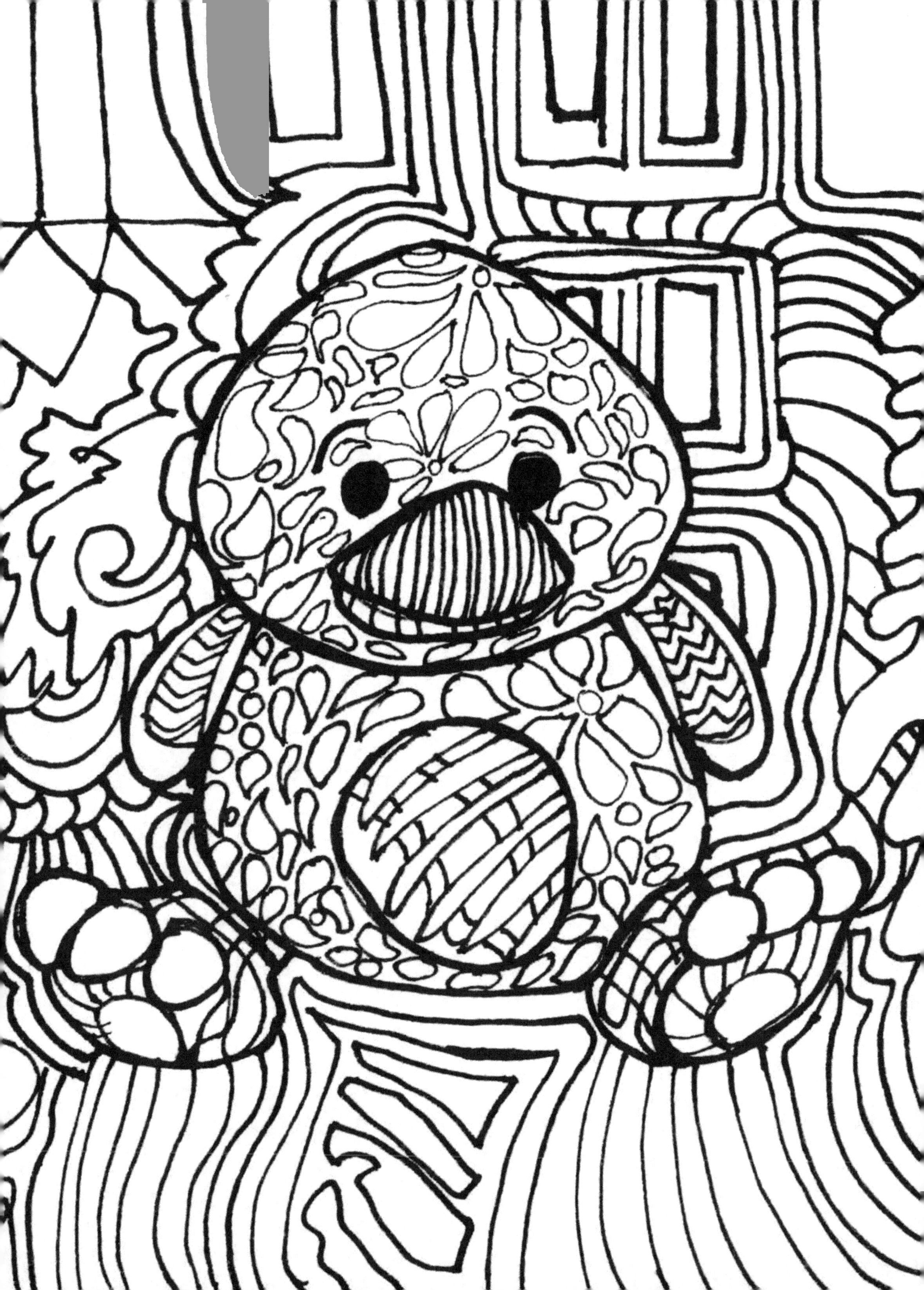

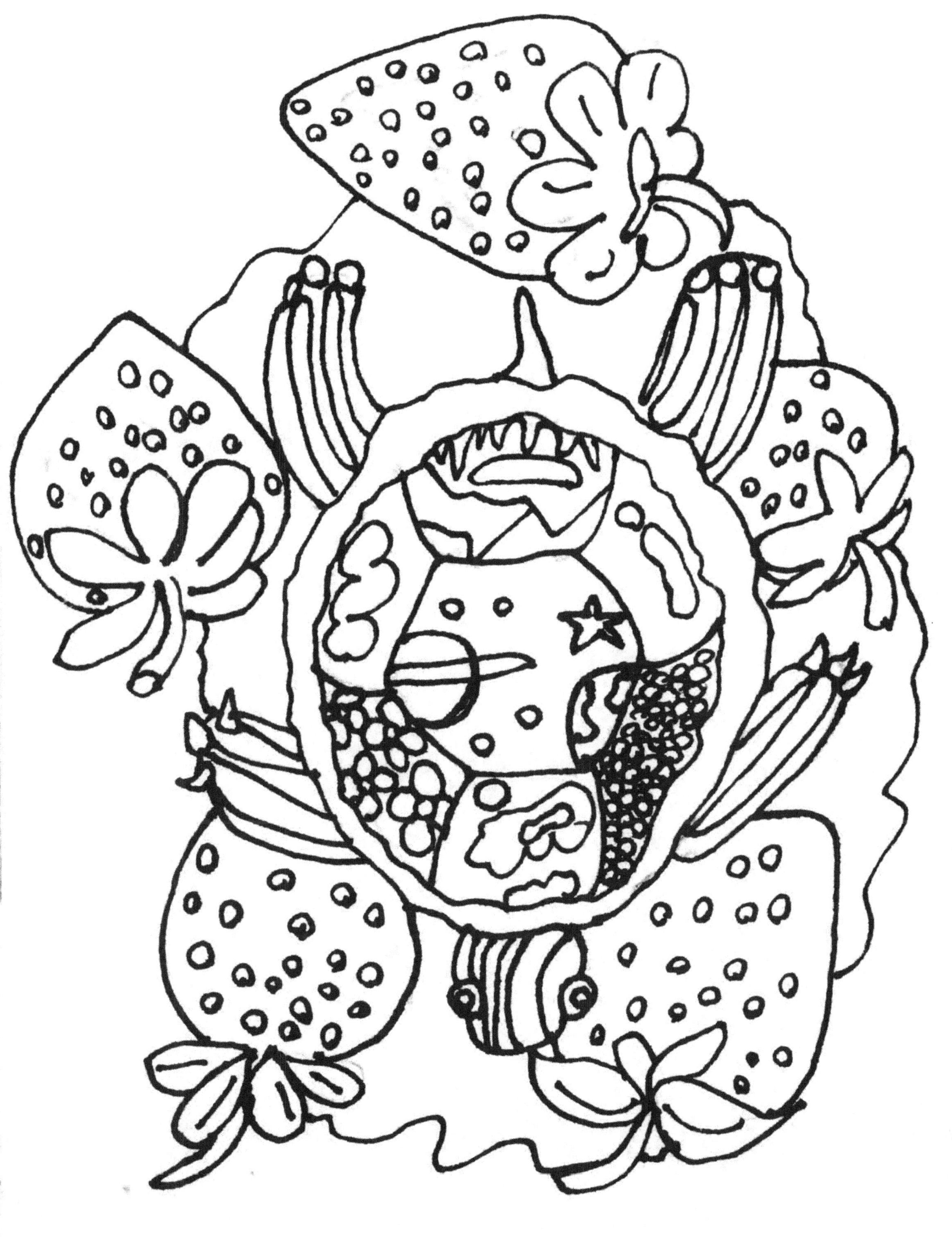

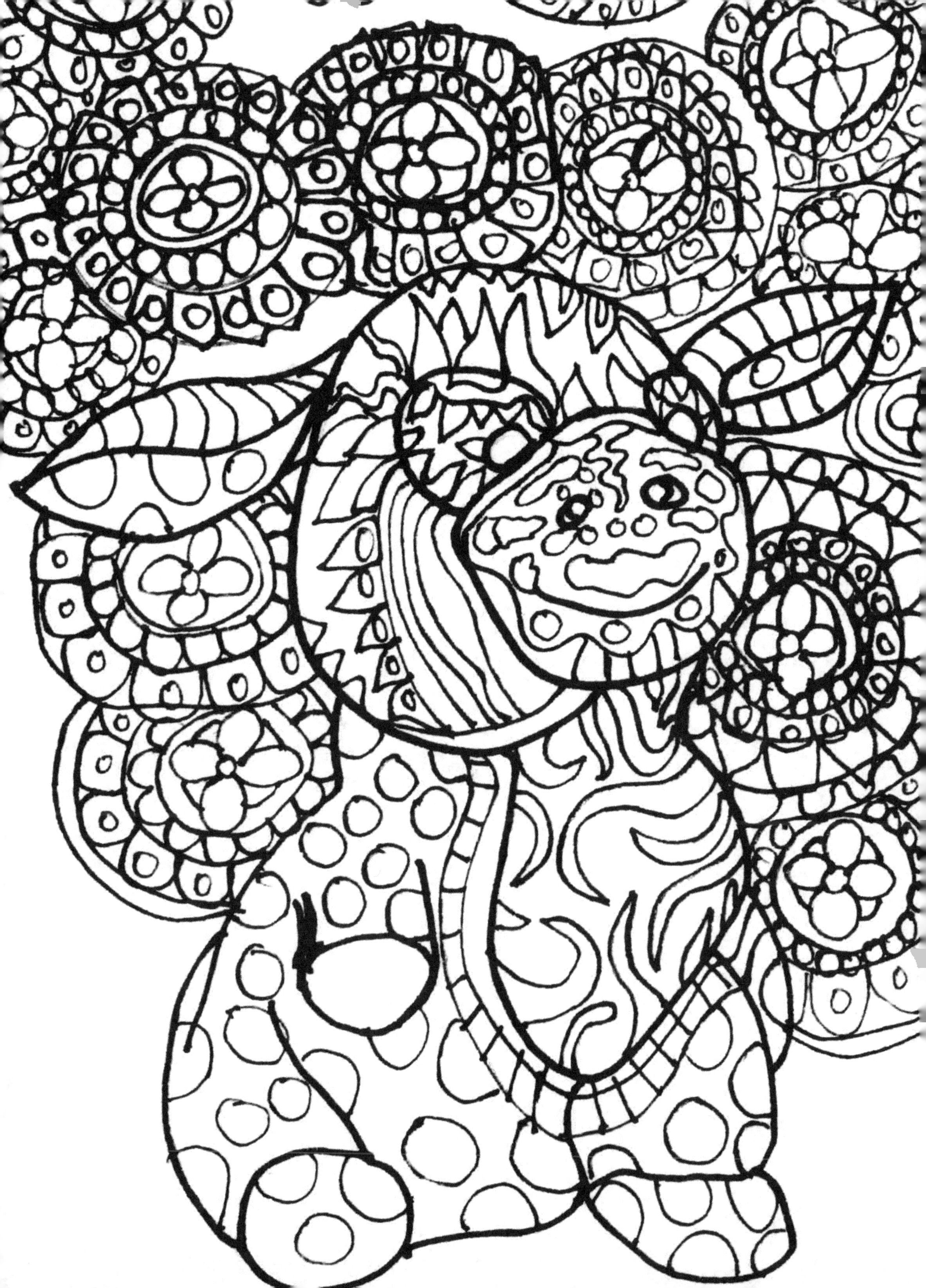

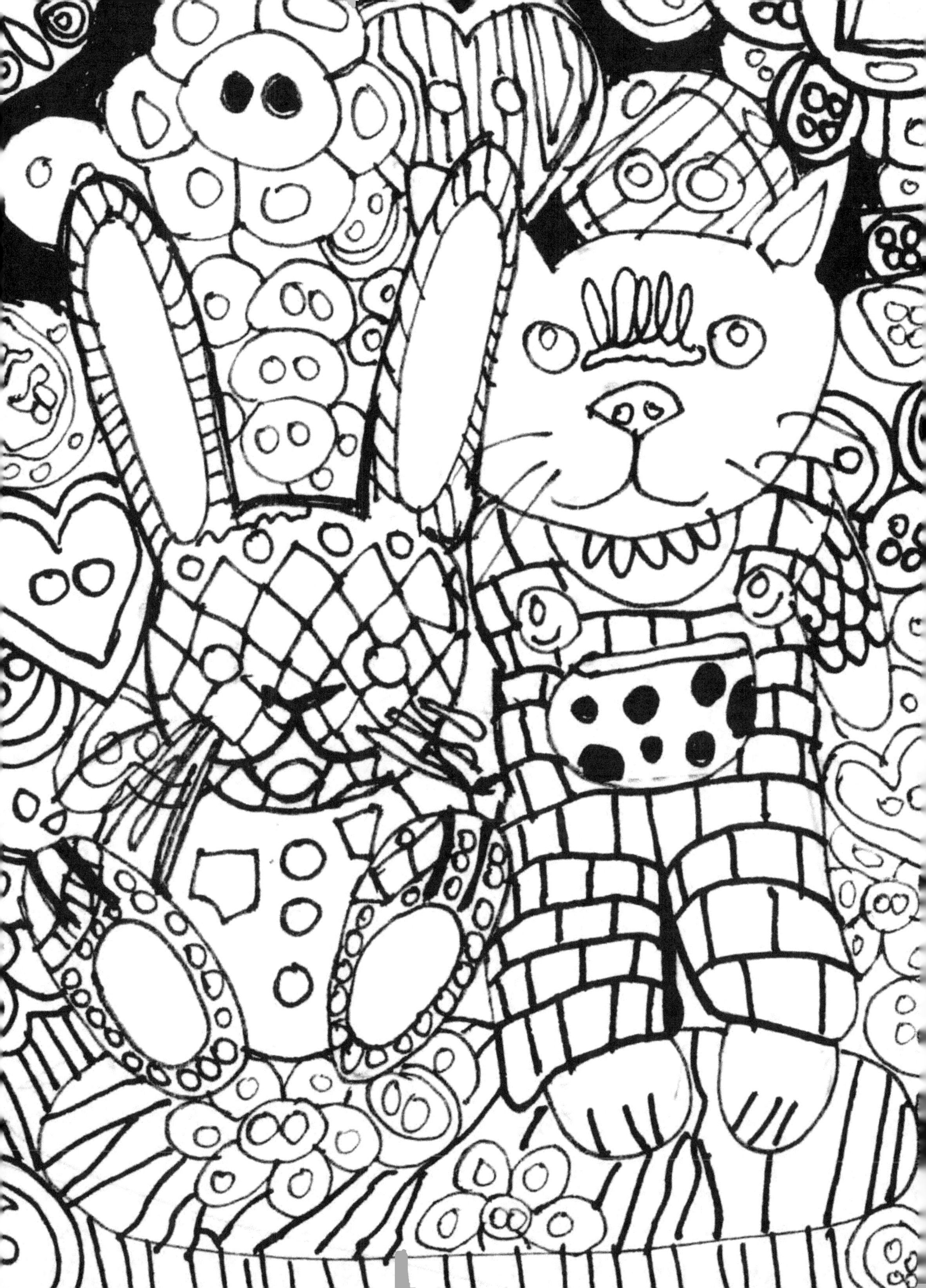

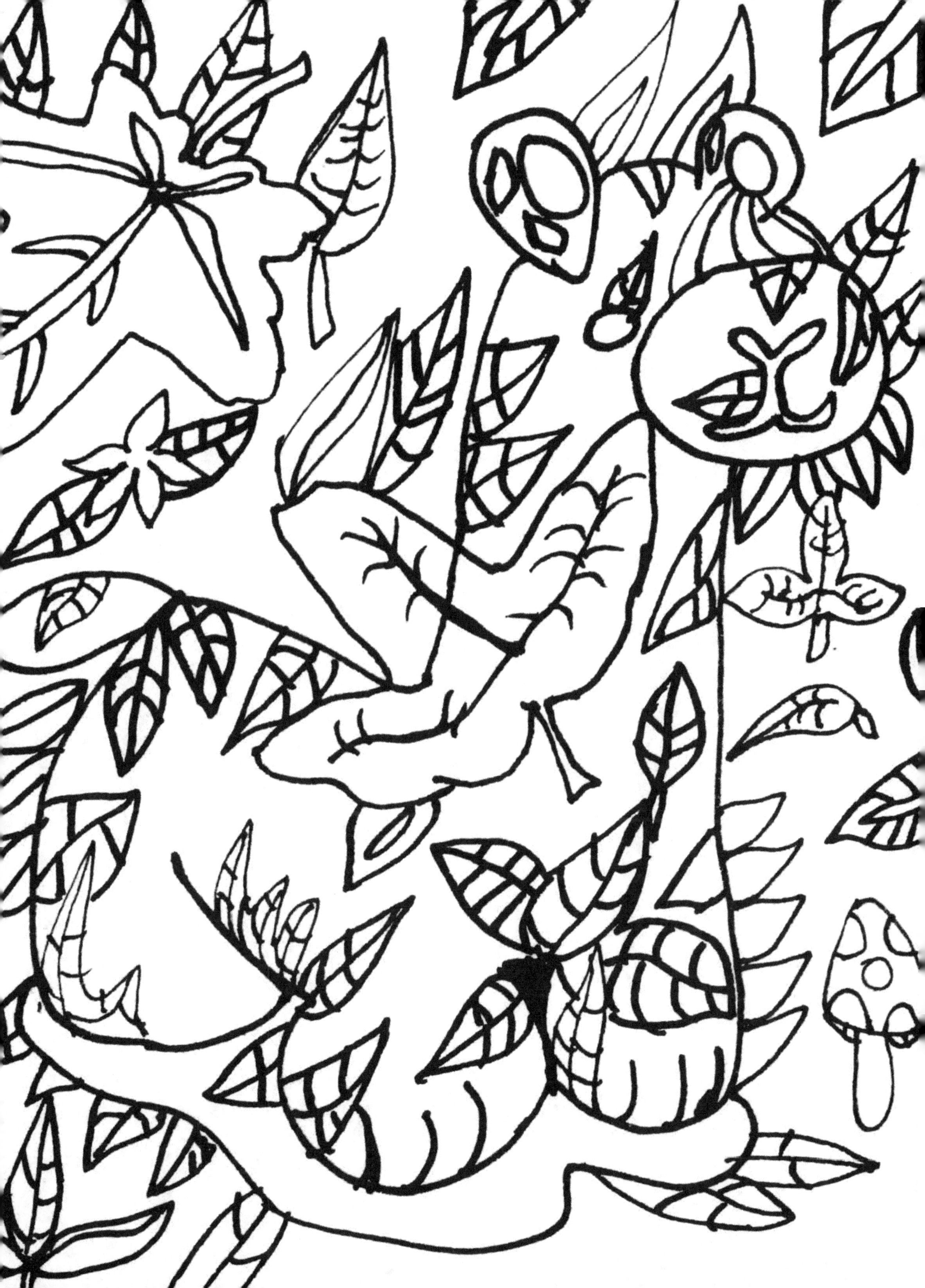

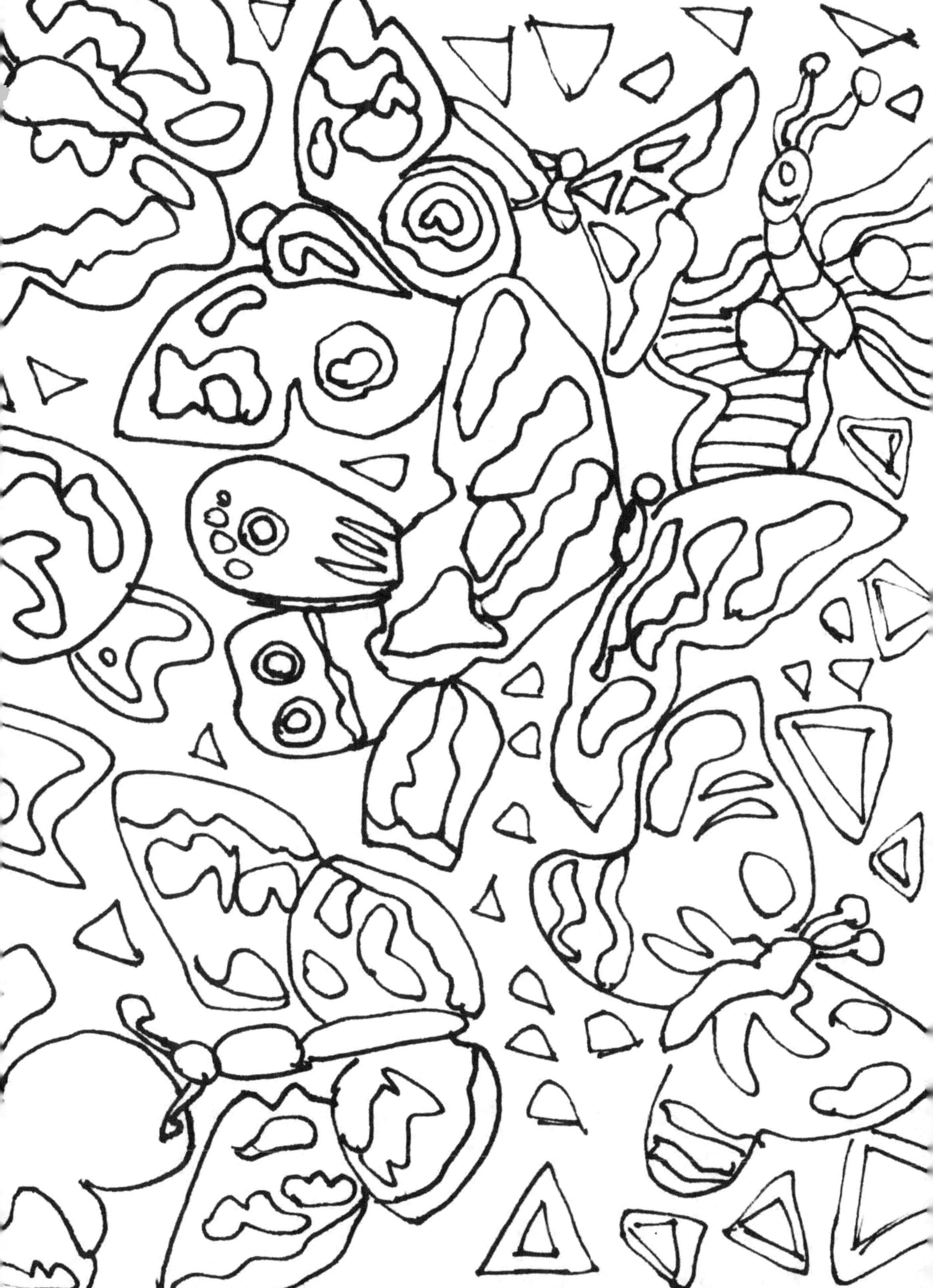

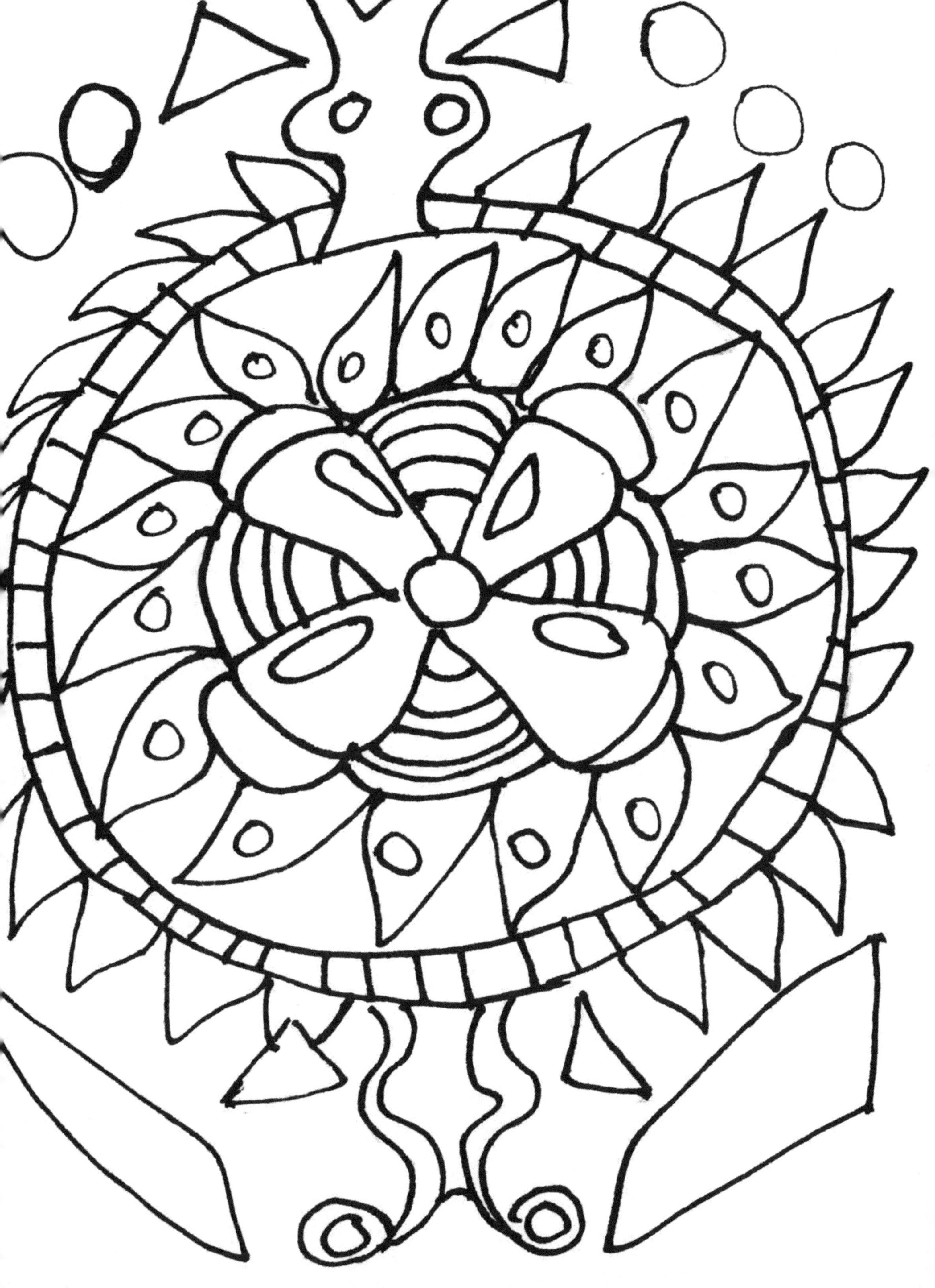

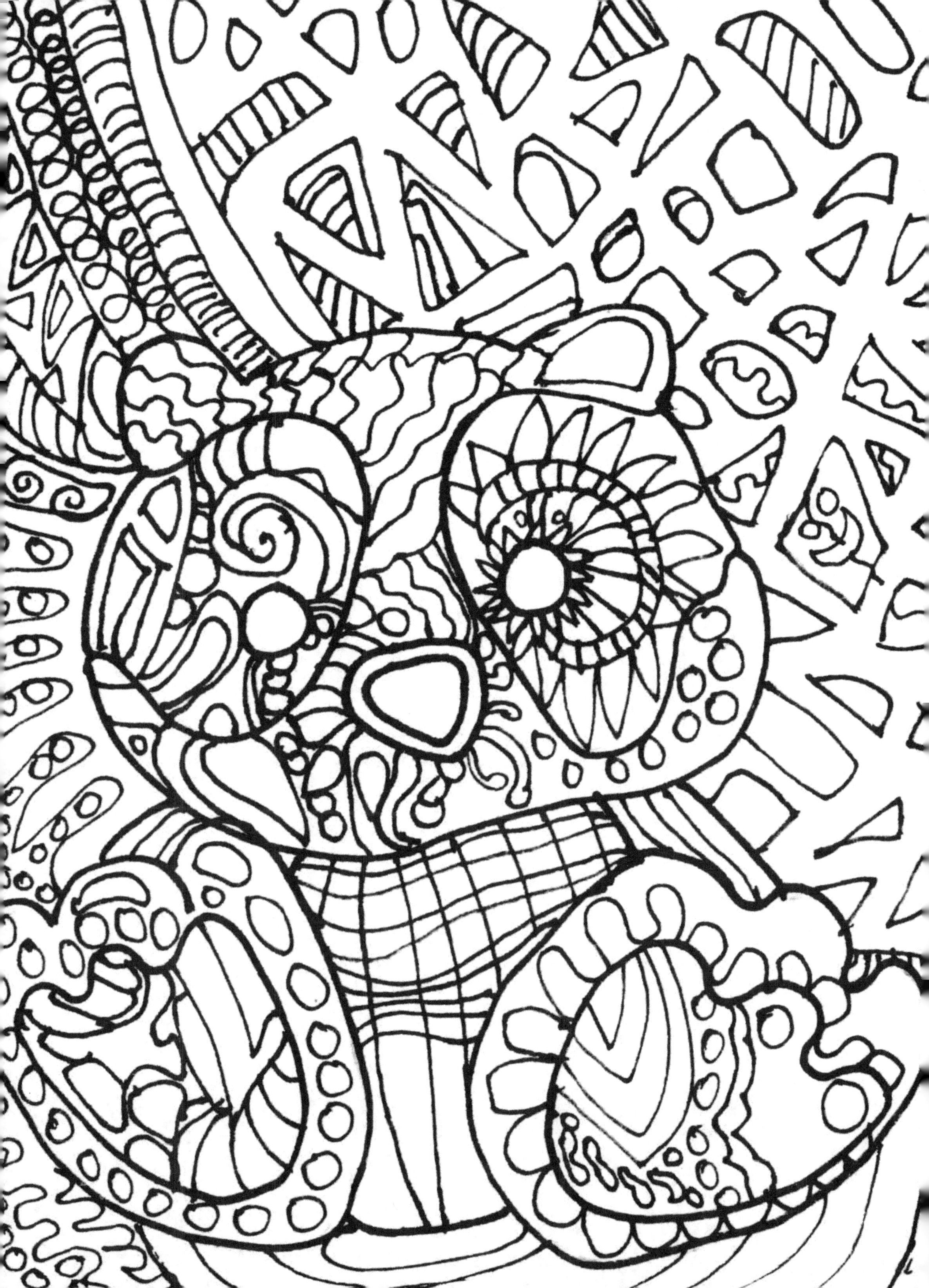

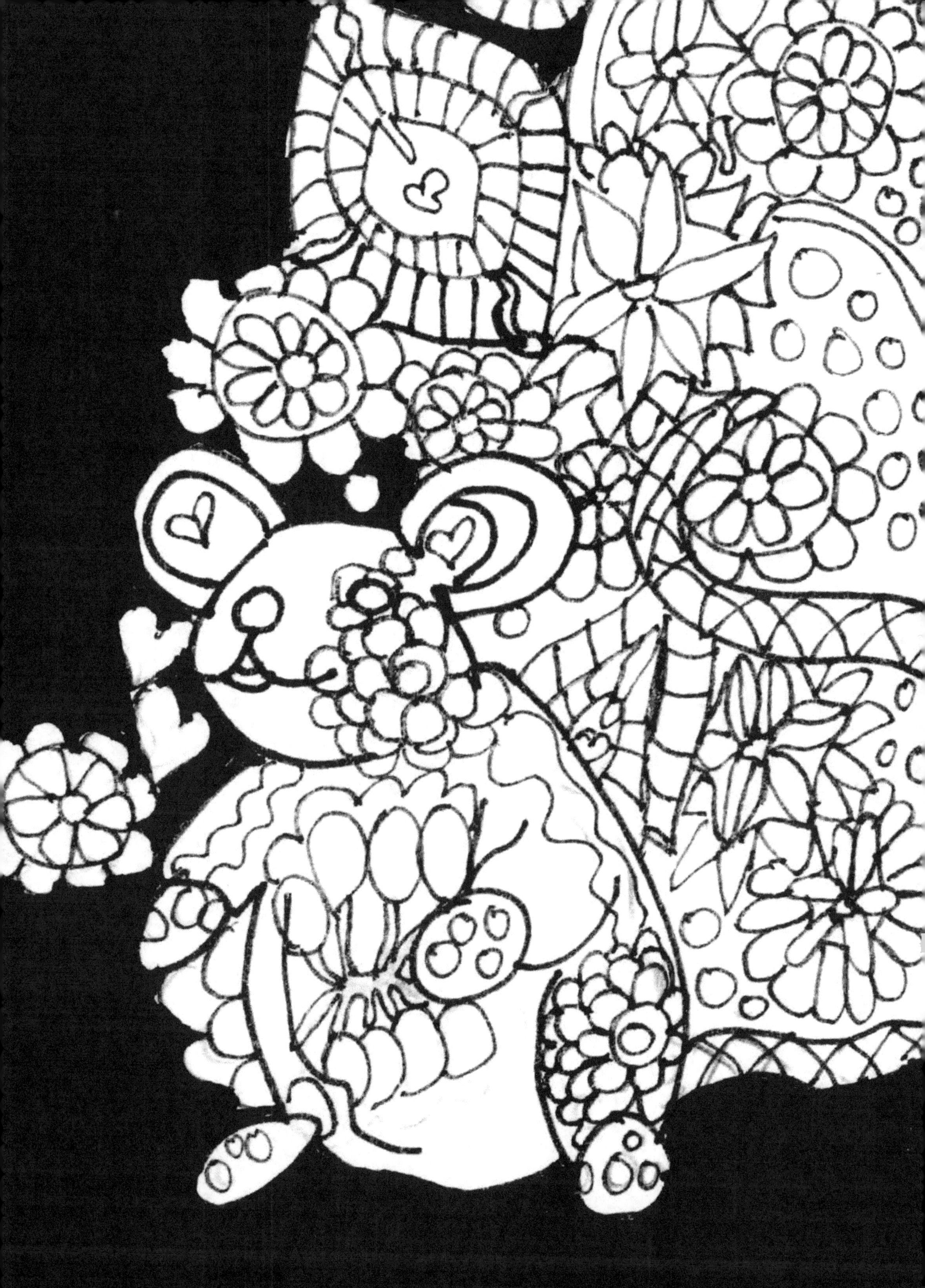

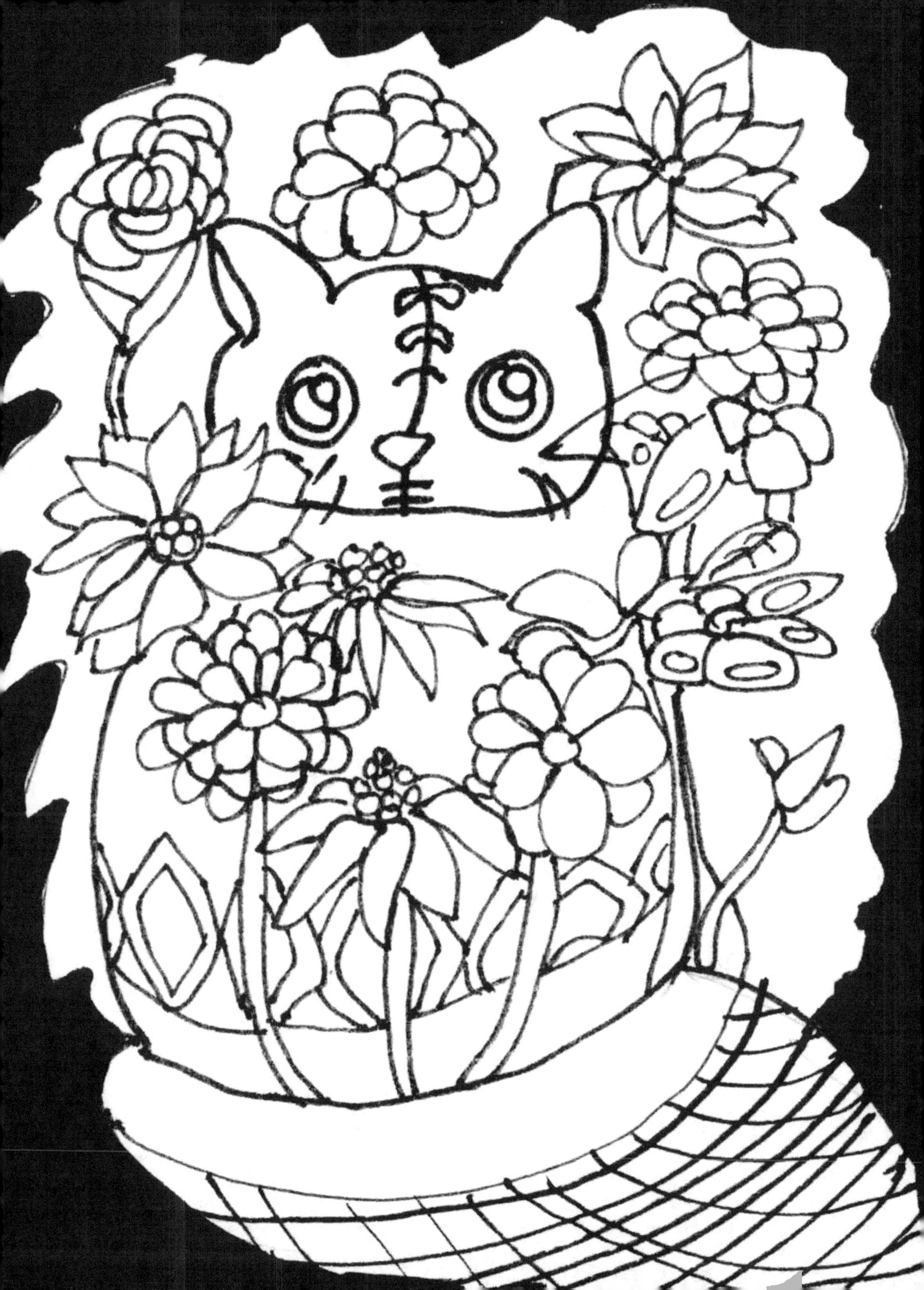

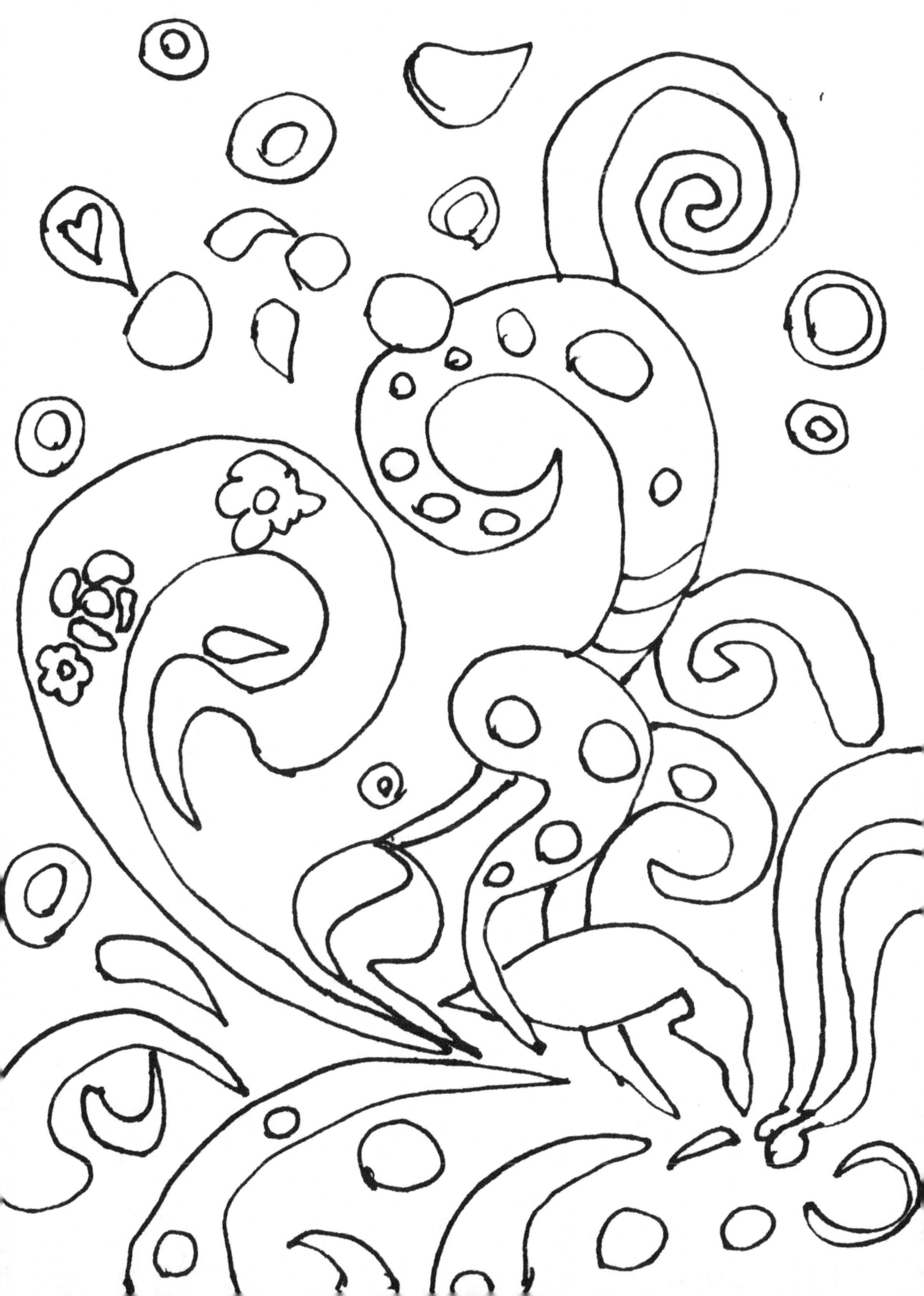

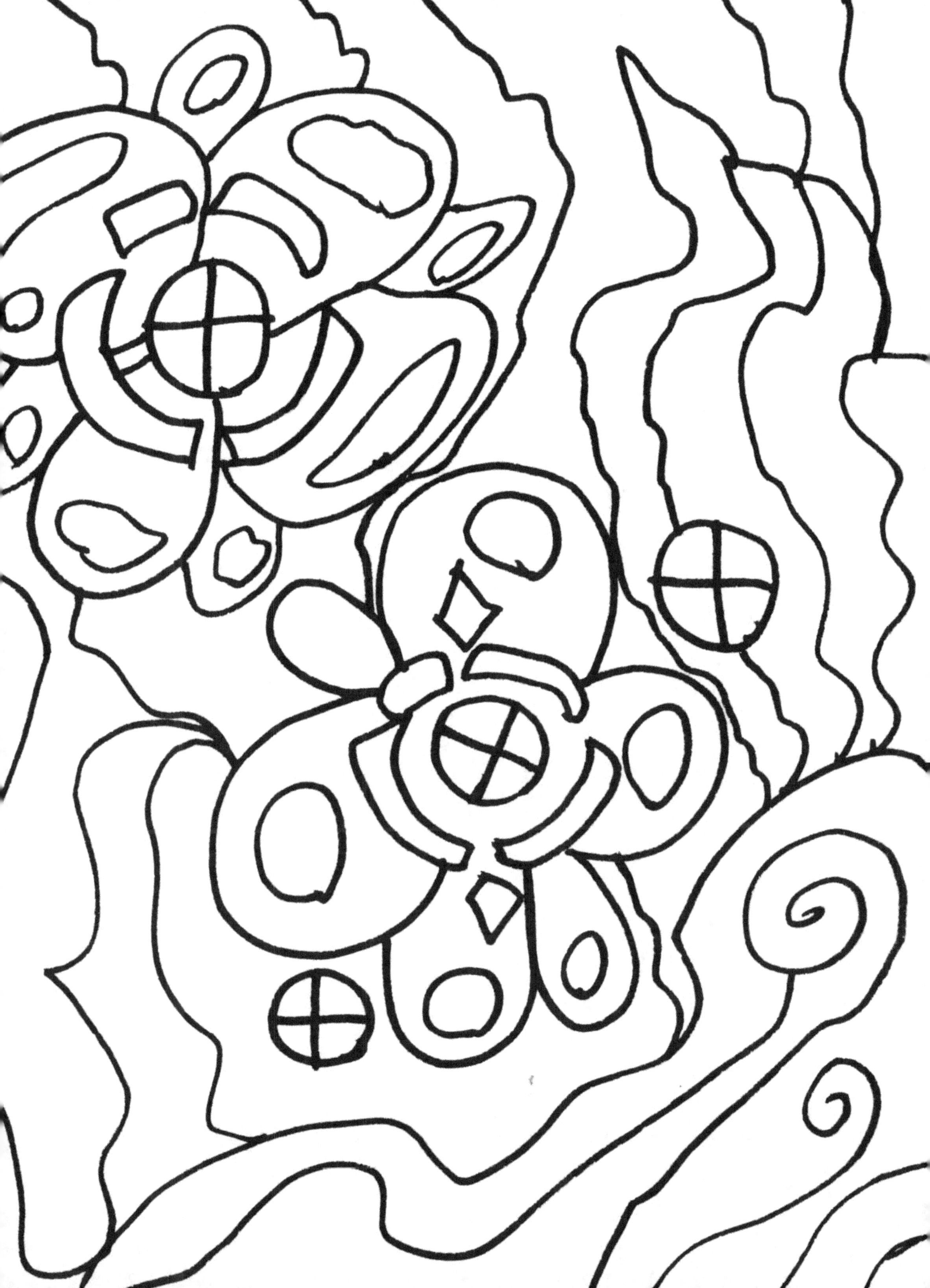

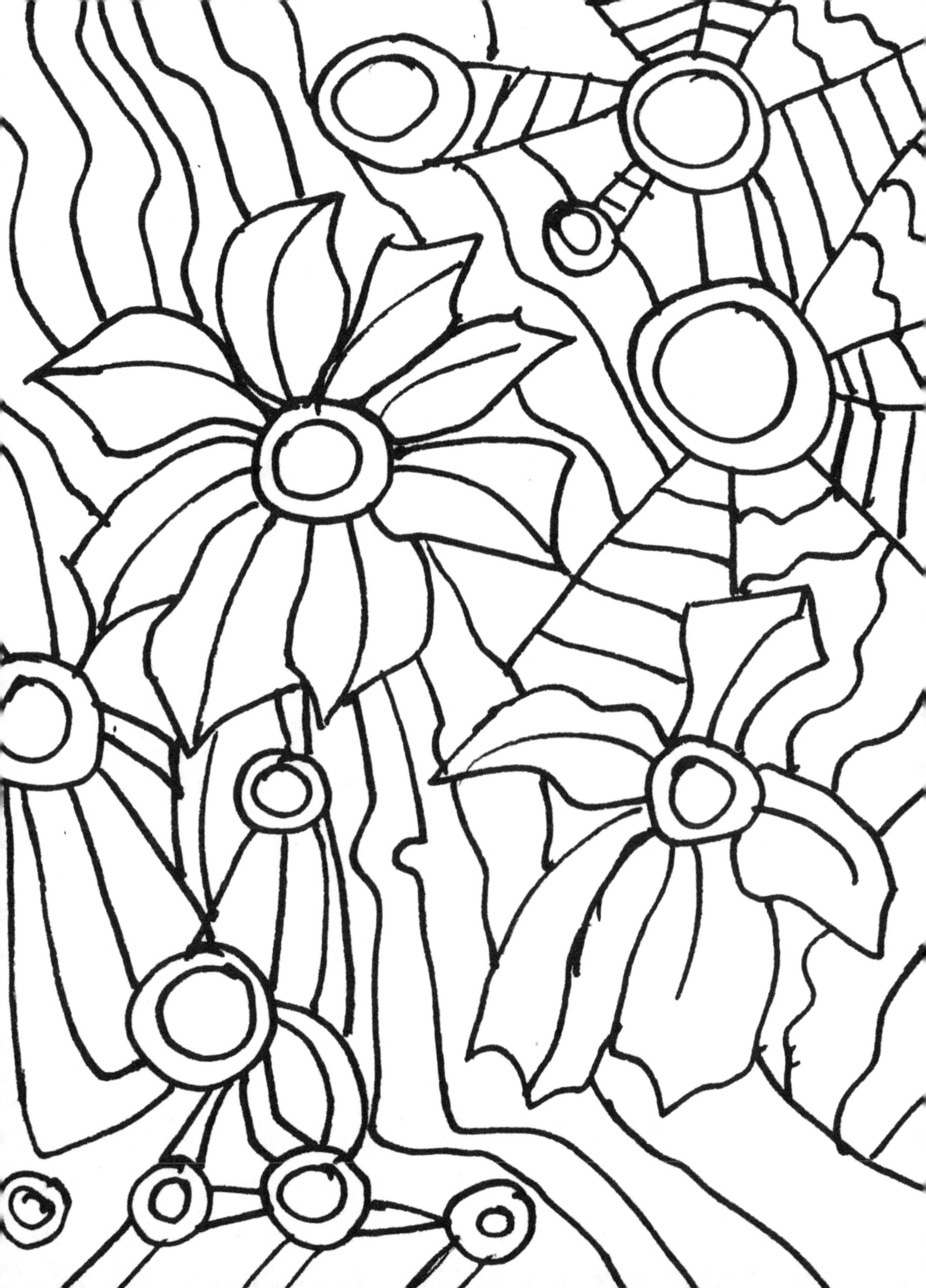

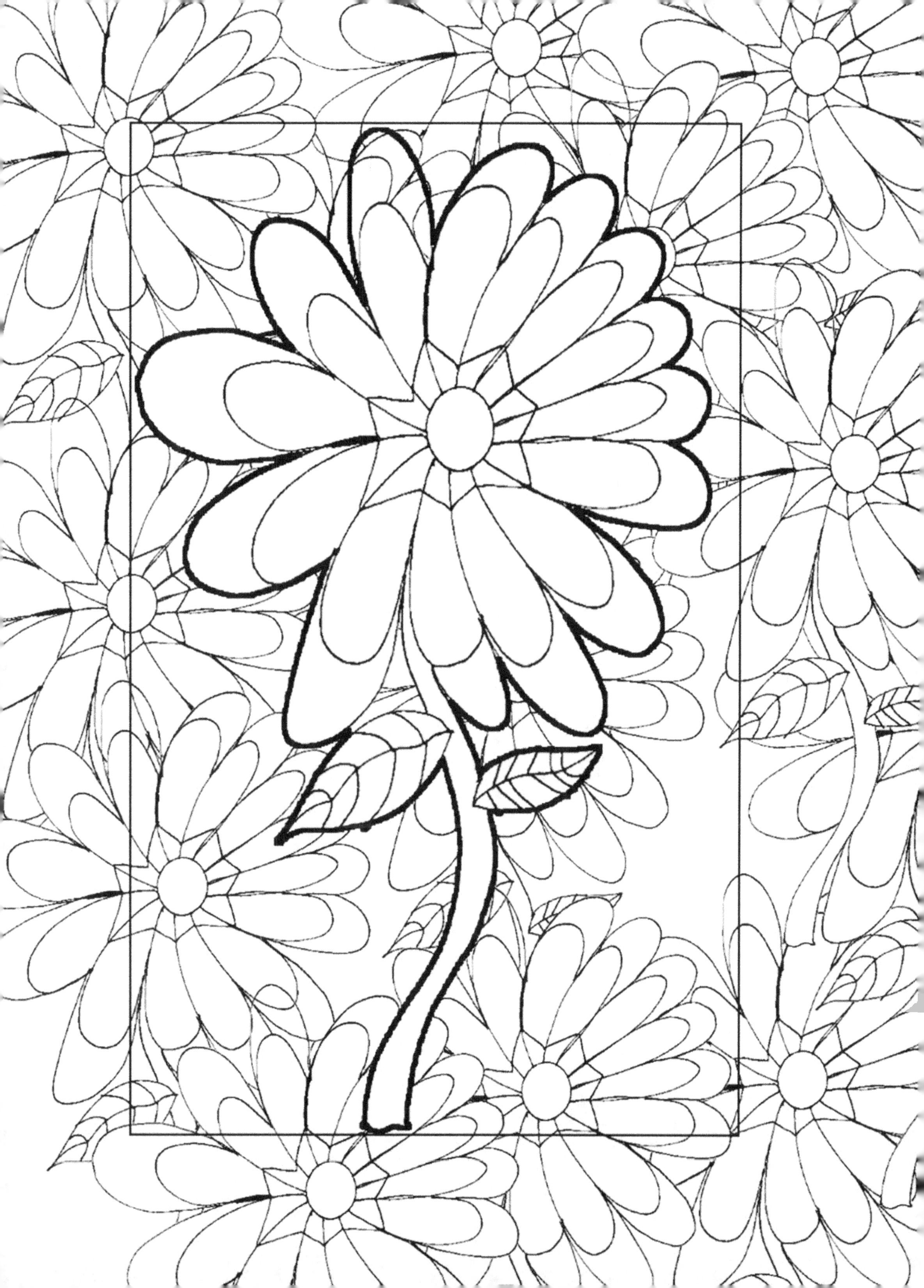

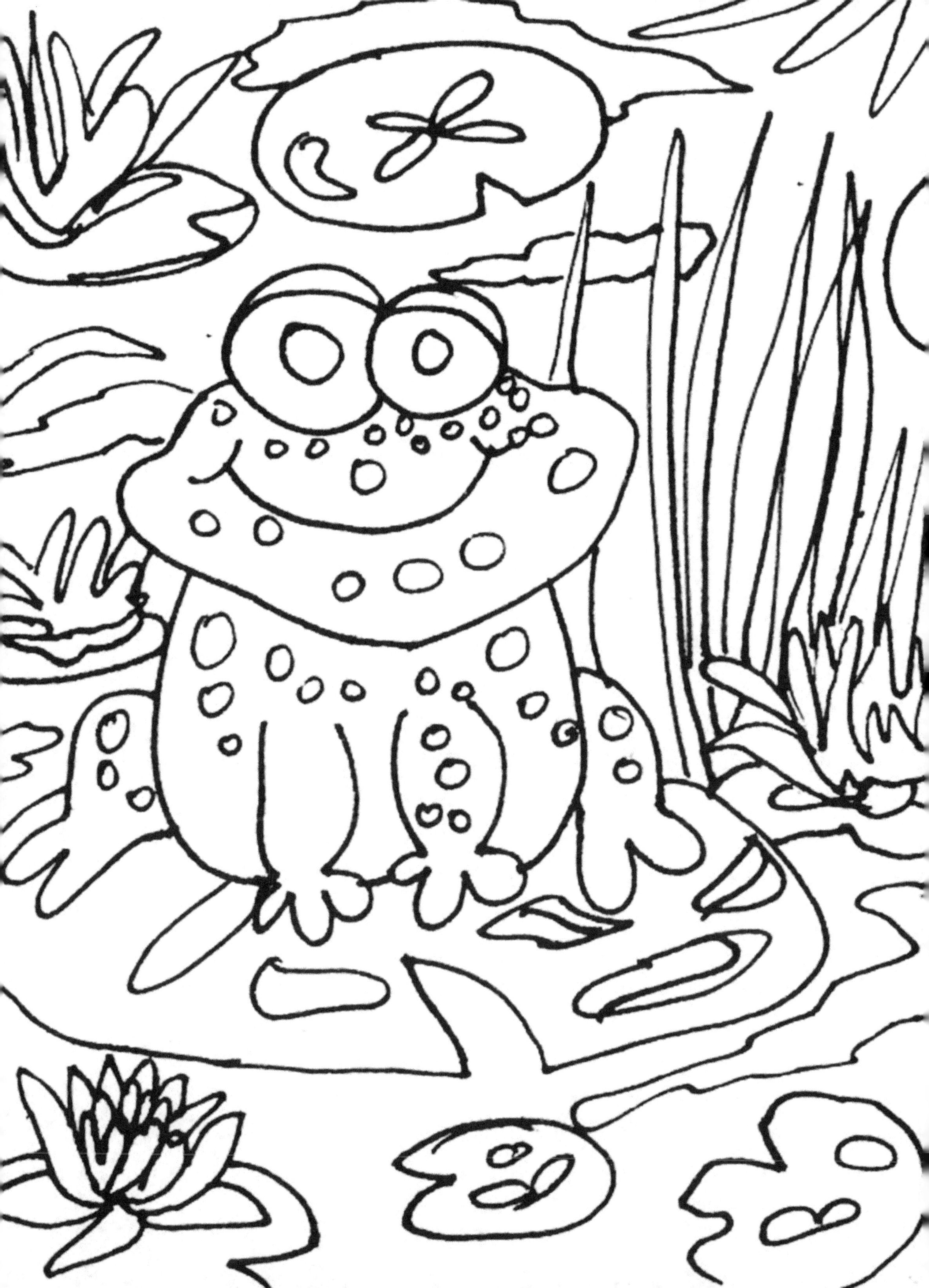

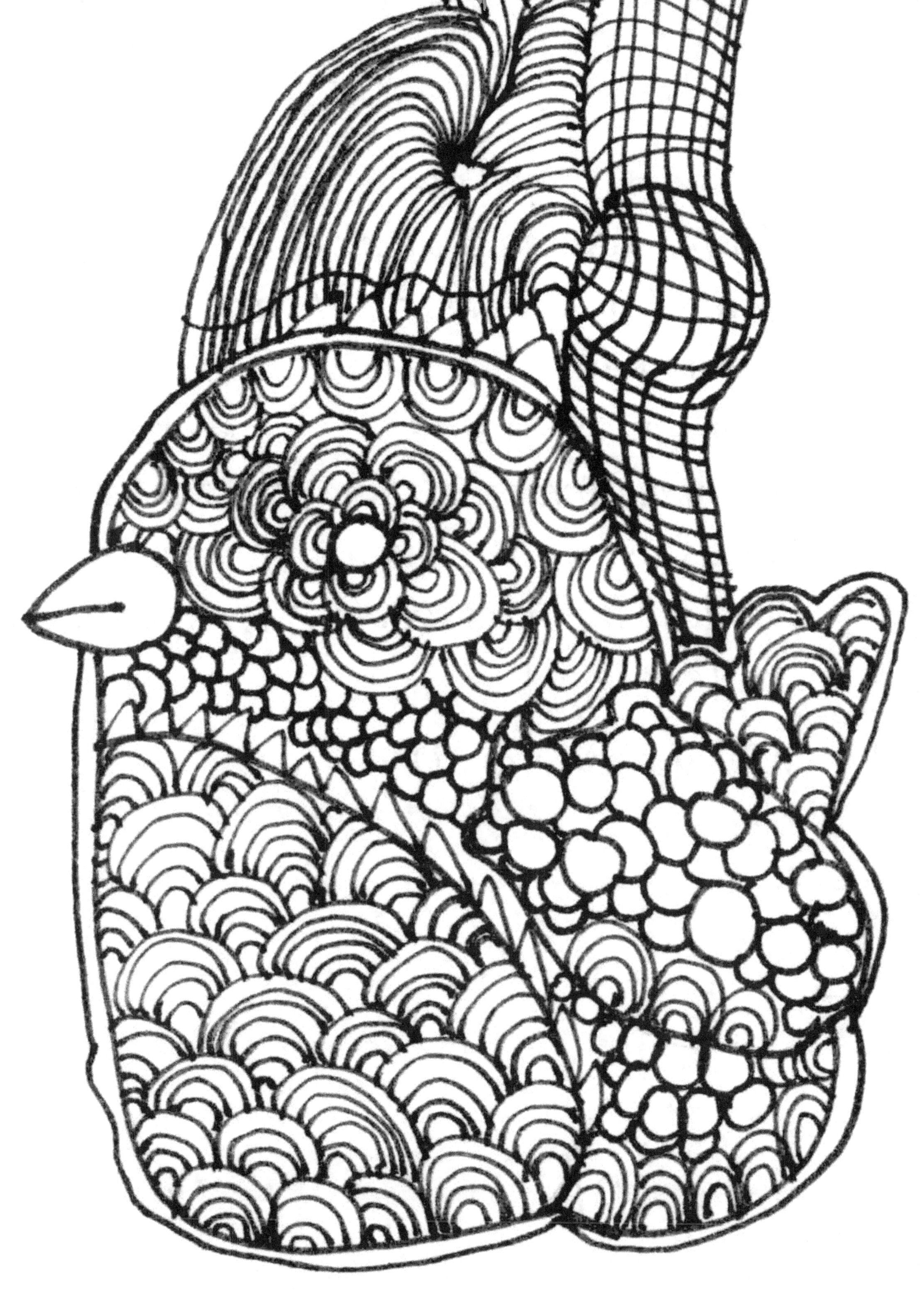

Thank you so much for purchasing Animal Jungle coloring book! I hope you really enjoyed it! I would love a review from you! So please, let me know what you liked and didn't like about my book! I'm listening. ❤❤ your comments will impact my next book! Your opinion matters to me!

WWW.Kaylinart.Org

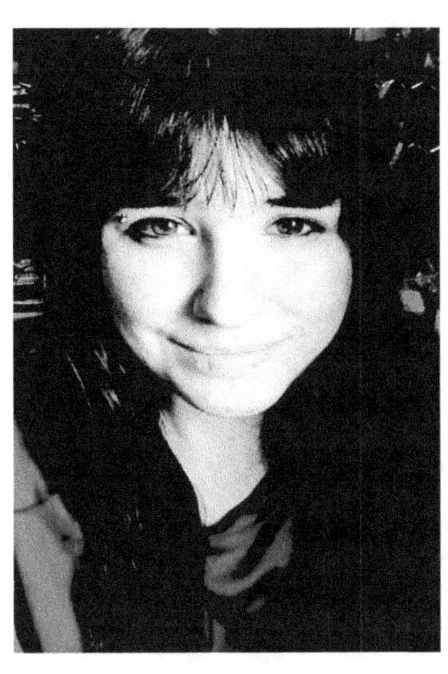

About Me

My name is Lin Watchorn I am a Freelance Artist and Author. I've won multiple art shows and have been recognized in the art field for my unique and dark drawings. I love the outdoors and mountains of Utah! I spend most of my time Drawing, writing, running, cycling and teaching myself new skills!

Contact me:

Facebook:
https://www.facebook.com/Kaylin-Watchorn-Art

Email: LinWatchorn@rocketmail.com

Join my FREE email list, for prizes and giveaways! Also updates on my books!

http://eepurl.com/bD8HzX

Instagram: Kaylinart

Twitter: KaylinArtist

Pinterest: Linwatchorn

TSU: www.tsu.co/kaylinart